INTRODU

There is something about the numb
United. Once in a while, whoever dons the blood red shirt with this magical digit on the back becomes possessed by an unquantifiable power that takes the game of football into the realms of fantasy. Traditionally, squad numbers were used to distinguish and identify players and were also used to indicate the position of the player on the field. The origins of the number seven merely suggested that you played in the outside right position, however, as history will prove, this has not been the case for Manchester United.

The number seven jersey now has iconic status at Old Trafford. It can be Achilles' armour for some, a wearable Excalibur, a powerful jersey which makes some players look almost immortal. It can also be to burden for some, with lesser players unable to bare the weight of this numerical expectation. Mythology tells us that there are seven heavens, with the Sun, the Moon and five planets visible to the naked eye. What Manchester United fans have seen over the years from their own number sevens, has also been unmistakably out of this world.

A regular poser from the Old Trafford faithful for many years has been 'who will be the next number seven?' This has been a conundrum for many associated with Manchester United, including the great Sir Alex Ferguson, who in the latter stages of his management saw the significance of the shirt and handed it out with a mixture of caution and expectation. This trend has now continued with the managers that have followed.

Some players ask for the exalted shirt, some players refuse it. Some players excel wearing the number seven, and others fail to live up to the iconography associated with it, however, every so often a footballer comes along to make the jersey his own.

It is difficult to say whether they found the shirt, or the shirt found them. What we do know is the number has been worn by some of the greatest players ever to grace the Theatre of Dreams; players who have taken the club to a celestial level, men who have inspired his team to do the improbable. This is the Legends of the Number Seven.

GEORGE BEST

I think I've found a genius

It is often said that the soul of Manchester United Football Club was embodied and personified during the era of the Busby Babes. The paradox is that the players who first embraced the birth of this conceptualisation were soon lost in the tragic death of the Munich Air Disaster. However what became absent in person, still remained in philosophy and spirit. Why this quest for re-enactment has remained football's most powerful footballing philosophy and why the thesis has become as enigmatic as it has remains open to analysis. To explain the concept of the spirit of Manchester United and its genesis would be as unquantifiable as explaining the origins of the universe. A prevalent offshoot of this doctrine is Manchester United's number seven shirt. This phenomenon is one of the components which embodies the Nuclei of Manchester United Football Club; and its original notable recipient in the post-Munich era was first discovered in the in the shadows of Belfast.

Manchester United's scouting network heading into the sixties was still in full force despite the tragedy of the Busby Babes. After a few years of patching up his squad, Matt Busby persisted with his search for young home-grown talent in an attempt to reignite the club as one of Europe's greatest once more. The mission to find players who could replicate the likes Duncan Edwards, Tommy Taylor and Billy Whelen seemed an unachievable ask, as a team of such quality were surely a 'once in a generation' occurrence. However, a telegram which the manager received in 1961 from Manchester United scout Bob Bishop suggested that perhaps the club had found a once in a generation player, as upon the discovery of George Best, Bishop wrote the spine-tingling words 'I think I've found a genius'.

George Best's prodigal displays in United's youth ranks saw him fast-tracked into the team at the age of 17. His debut came against

West Bromwich Albion at Old Trafford on 14th September 1963 where United won 1-0. He was given the number seven shirt, indicating that he would start in the outside right position, yet as the game progressed he drifted from either side of the pitch, displaying his attacking prowess to the home crowd. His starting position saw him matched-up against West Brom defender Graham Williams, who's no-nonsense style encouraged him to kick Best out of the game. But the young Irishman showed something that was not expected to be seen that day, which was courage in abundance. He would be continually knocked-down by hardened professionals, yet bounce back up and continue playing. His all-round display was nerveless, he played with no fear and nothing fazed him. If his talent was said to be prodigious, then his bravery was unequivocal.

For the remainder of the year Best continued to learn his trade for Manchester United in the A and B Leagues, before being recalled to the first team at the end of December. United had been thrashed 6-1 by Burnley at Turf Moor on Boxing Day causing (a then knightless) Matt Busby to make changes for the reverse fixture two days later at Old Trafford. George was celebrating Christmas with his family at the time, yet the last-minute call-up saw him fly over for the match the day before. United rectified their defeat with a 5-1 win, with number eleven George Best scoring the Red's third goal in an all-round performance, with flashes genius and an abundance of desire. Best flew back to Belfast the night after the game to be reunited back with his family, with many forgetting that despite his ability on the football pitch, he was still a teenager who struggled to part with his family and friends.

Despite this, there were no doubts in the managers mind, George Best was in the team. He became a regular starter for the Reds and it was on January 18th 1964 away to West Brom that another footballing portent emerged from what appeared to be a run of the mill league match. Bobby Charlton, a Munich survivor had become an instrumental part of Matt Busby's team, and together with several new signings including Scottish centre-forward Denis Law, Busby had accrued a team which were capable of competing for silverware once more. As United travelled to the Hawthorns it emerged, somewhat innocuously that Best, Law and Charlton would start a football match alongside each other for the fist time. The story of the day was that these three players would all score in a 4-1 win, with George Best rounding off a comprehensive victory with United's fourth goal. After the match it was the names of these three players which were written and spoken about in awe; and the sight of them playing together on the same pitch was unknowingly the greatest prognostic symbol to ever grace a football field.

Best's next goal came in a 4-0 win away to Burnley in the F.A. Cup fifth round on 15th February 1964, then two days later he scored two goals in a 5-0 league victory over Bolton Wanderers. Two weeks later United's defence of the F.A. Cup, which they had won the previous year, saw George score in a thrilling 3-3 draw against Sunderland in the quarter-final. The Reds progressed after a second replay, however, defeat to West Ham in the semi-final at Hillsbrough followed by an exit from the European Cup Winners' Cup four days later at the hands of Sporting Lisbon, meant that a good finish in the league was all Best could hope for in his first season. United eventually finished runners-up, with the young Irishman only missing two matches since his reintroduction and his influence meant he was now one of United's key players at the age of only eighteen. Another milestone for the season was an F.A. Youth Cup victory, with George being part of the winning team. This was the sixth time that United had won the competition with Jimmy Murphy in charge and it was also the first time they had won it since the Munich air disaster six years earlier.

In the 1964/65 season George Best became a first choice member of the team, predominately playing in the outside left position which meant he would be wearing the number eleven shirt. Manchester United were slow out of the blocks in this campaign, however their first win of season came at Old Trafford on September 2nd 1964 with a 3-1 victory over West Ham United. George Best scored the third goal for the Reds that day, as the Holy Trinity of Best, Charlton and Law played rings around the Hammers' defence. Yet United lost their next match away to Fulham and then after drawing the following game against Everton at Goodison Park, their league title winning ambitions seemed to be minimised. Then a 3-0 home win over Nottingham Forest, followed by a 2-1 victory over Everton at Old Trafford, where

Best scored United's opening goal, saw United kick start a run of 18 games without a defeat in the league and cup. United were not just winning these matches, they were pulverising their opponents at times. They scored 34 goals in a run of performances that had not been seen since the days preceding the Busby Babes' fateful trip back from Belgrade. During this run, George Best netted in a 2-0 win away to Chelsea in late September after latching onto a stray back pass, before setting up Denis Law with a tantalising cross for him to head in the second. He then scored in a 6-1 drubbing of Djurgardens in the second leg of the Inter-Cities Fairs Cup first round second leg on October 27th 1964, when he blasted the ball home from the edge of the box to send Manchester United through to the second round of the competition 7-2 on aggregate.

Two weeks later United faced Borussia Dortmund in the first leg of this tie at Old Trafford, with the Belfast forward repeating his heroics with another solo goal and and all-round mesmeric performance in another 6-1 win, before United won the return leg in Germany 4-0. In between these matches, Best added another goal to his tally in a 3-0 victory over Blackburn Rovers at Old Trafford, before ending the year on a high with the winning goal against Sheffield United at Bramall Lane on Boxing Day. United's first game of the calendar year saw Best score their opening goal against Chester City in the F.A. Cup third round. The Reds then progressed to the quarter-finals of the Inter-Cities Fairs Cup with a two-legged win over Everton, either side of a replayed F.A. Cup win over Stoke City.

George Best then scored in a 3-2 victory over Burnley on February 13th 1965. However his contribution to beating Burnley 2-1 in the F.A. Cup fifth round a week later was even more remarkable. With United trailing 1-0 and with time running out, Best appeared to be having trouble with his left boot, so the impudent teenager decided to see out the remainder of the match with one of his boots in his hand. With five minutes left on the clock, Best swung in a cross with his left sock, which bounced in the air for Law to acrobatically equalise with an over-head kick. Best then provided the assist for United's winner, this time with his booted right foot, which set-up Paddy Crerand to score from long-range. United then took part in a 5-3 thriller against Wolverhampton Wanderers at Molineux, where

George Best was once again amongst the scorers, after sliding home United's third goal to put them in front after Wolves took a 2-0 lead.

George Best's ability to change the boundaries of what was capable on the football pitch had reached a new apex of rebellion. His gravity defying movement across the grass and his ability to beat defenders was revolutionary; and his actions on the field were conducive to those wishing to break the cultural mould in the self-liberated and expressive era of the 1960's.

The Northern Irishman had now established himself as one of United's most fearsome players, however, as with many young footballers in the sixties, the opposition perhaps looked to exploit his age and inexperience. It was feared that as the season reached its important stages, the pressure of expectation and the brutality of English football's centre-halves could take its toll on the teenager.

On March 3rd 1965 United faced Chelsea in a league match which was crucial to the title race, as Chelsea, who were leading the table at this point came to Old Trafford to put a mark on their fellow challengers. Yet it was United who sailed into a two goal lead after a brace from David Herd. George Best then displayed more of his repertoire when he charged down a clearance from the Chelsea full back Eddie McCreadie. After showing bravery in the challenge, he then lobbed the ball over McCreadie's head, before setting the defender into a panic when Best's harrying caused the Chelsea number three to collapse on the floor in confusion. Best then nicked the ball off his opponent before executing an inch perfect chip over Peter Bonetti in the Chelsea goal. It was sheer craftsmanship from player whose talent was starting to have no boundaries.

It was also a demonstration that this player could not be intimidated by rough-house tactics; on the contrary, it was now the opposition that were beginning to be afraid of him. United lost to Leeds United in the F.A. Cup semi-final after a replay, yet they managed to exact revenge on their Yorkshire rivals by winning 9 of their last 11 league games meaning that Sir Matt Busby's men pipped Leeds to the Division One title on goal difference. Their season concluded with a 1-0 semi-final play-off loss to Ferencvaros in the Inter-Cities' Fairs Cup, despite cruising past Strasbourg 5-0 in the previous round. Despite this, United were the newly crowned champions of England and George Best was the newest young starlet to emerge from Sir Matt Busby's seemingly infinite pool of youth. The youngster missed only one match throughout the entire campaign; and after conquering England, United and a young Best now set their sights on conquering Europe.

O Quinto Beatle

Manchester United started the season with a 2-2 draw against Liverpool in the Charity Shield, which was held at Old Trafford. George Best opened the scoring for the Reds as the trophy was shared between the two north-west rivals. Their league campaign had a stuttering start as the reigning champions could only muster two league wins in their first eight games. Best's first league goal of the campaign came in a 4-2 defeat to Nottingham Forest in early September. Then the nineteen-year-old set his sights on the European Cup. The Reds overcome HJK Helsinki 3-2 in the Preliminary Round first leg in Finland, before inflicting a 6-0 Drubbing over the Finnish Champions at Old Trafford, where Best scored the first European Cup goal of his career.

George Best then made his next appearance in the Manchester United number seven shirt against Blackburn Rovers on November 6th 1965 in a 2-2 draw at Old Trafford. The only short-term significance at the time was that Best switched to the outside right position, allowing Johnny Aston to occupy the outside left position which gave a more natural balance to the team. At this point, the number seven shirt bore no significance apart from the ease in which the player could be identified by the supporters and commentators, together with the tradition of the player's position. Yet unbeknown to Manchester United, the number switch which occurred this day would have an earth-shattering effect on the footballing world. George Best had reacquired the number seven shirt by virtue of a positional change on the field. However this day would be the first step towards a historic change in the folklore of Manchester United.

Best then scored his first goal as a number seven in the following match away to Leicester City, where United beat the home side 5-0.

Towards the end of a rampant Manchester United display, Crerand passed the ball to Best who mesmerised two defenders on the edge of the box, leaving two of them sprawled on the deck by sheer body movement, before rifling home Manchester United's fifth. When George Best dribbled the ball it was as if the Earth moved and he stood still. Defenders would end-up horizontal on the turf with one flick of a hip. His movement was as subtle as a lamb, yet the aftershock for the defenders was seismic.

Best then added two more goals to his total with a double strike against Sheffield United at Old Trafford. Either side of this match, United progressed to the quarter-finals of the European Cup after a 5-1 aggregate victory over ASK Vorwaerts, before Best added another goalscoring brace against Sunderland at Roker Park on December 11th 1965. His first goal was immaculately driven in from 20 yards, before tapping in his second after good work from Bobby Charlton on the flank.

Four days later the teenager continued his goalscoring run after netting against Everton in a 3-0 home win, meaning George Best had now scored 6 goals in 5 games following his transition to the number seven role. He added three more goals to his ever-growing repertoire with a strike against Sunderland at Old Trafford in a 1-1 draw, before a double against Derby County in the F.A. Cup two weeks later. Then on March 5th 1966 United faced Wolves in the F.A. Cup at Molineux. The Reds found themselves 2-0 down after 9 minutes which meant victory was seemingly beyond them. Yet two goals by Law brought them back into the cup tie before George Best turned on his magic again. First he bravely intercepted a Wolves attack with a jumping block, before wriggling past three players on the half-way line. After playing a one-two with Kidd he then out-ran two defenders, before slotting the ball home past the helpless goalkeeper to astonishingly put the visitors 3-2 in front. The game ended 4-2 to United with Herd adding a fourth, yet it was the twinkle-toed Belfast boy who would be lauded once more after the match. George Best's football was now becoming a box-office, must-see event. Thousands of fans were now flocking to see Manchester United play just for a glimpse of the young Northern Irishman in action. He was drawing attention to himself like the headline act at a concert; and amidst the rock and roll scene of the swinging sixties, Best was now becoming the star of his own show.

Four days later on March 9th 1966 Manchester United travelled to Portugal to face Benfica at the Estadio Da Luz in the second leg of the European Cup quarter-final. After notching a 3-2 home leg victory a month earlier, United still had their work cut-out against the Portuguese champions, yet early in the game a free-kick by Tony Dunne was met by Best, who's brave header looped over the on-rushing Benfica goalkeeper Costa Pereira and into the goal. Then five minutes later, a long punt up field from Harry Gregg was headed down by David Herd into the path of Best, who's first touch left two of the opposing players for dead. George quickly soared past the last defender, then diverted the ball into the net before the goalkeeper could react. It was sheer choreographed artistry from George Best who had saved one of his finest performances for the European stage. This devastating solo act had now been witnessed first-hand by many of those oblivious to his name. Further goals from Connelly, Crerand and Charlton meant that United went on to win 5-1, which was all the more impressive as the home side had reached four of the five previous finals and boasted the current European Player of the Year, Eusabio. However, Best was the player of the moment and his back page glory was now transferable to to the front pages in the eyes of the media. The Portuguese press dubbed him 'O Quinto Beatle' meaning the Fifth Beatle, with his star quality and rock band haircut fitting the bill. Upon his return to England a photographer snapped the Belfast boy wearing a sombrero and the British press followed suit by using the headline 'El Beatle'. His comparison to the biggest band ever to come out of Britain was not just based on his appearance anymore. He now had the the fame and status as a comparison. He had all the attributes of a front-man in a rock band. He had the look, the skills, the showmanship; and like any good musician did before, it was now a footballer's turn to spread his growing reputation overseas. He became an unwitting pioneer overnight, as this was the origin of the first ever front-page footballer; and United's greatest post-war performance was the setting for Best's metamorphosis into a celebrity.

At the end of March, United progressed to the semi-finals of the F.A. Cup after beating Preston North End with a 3-1 replay win, however, this came at a price for Best as in the first match at Deepdale the youngster suffered a knee injury, which meant he only appeared in two matches during the remainder of the season with his leg heavily strapped. The Reds exited the European Cup in the last four after a 2-1 aggregate defeat to Partizan Belgrade, before losing 1-0 to Everton in the semi-final of the F.A. Cup. A decent run-in domestically saw them secure a fourth place finish in Division One, yet this season would still be remembered for George Best emerging as one of the most talented players ever to kick a football. In all, Best scored 17 goals in 43 appearances for the Reds before his campaign was cut short through injury.

The 1966/1967 season started with George Best scoring in United's opening game against West Bromwich Albion in a 5-3 win at Old Trafford, before lashing home a consolation goal from an acute angle after a through ball from Herd, against Leeds United a week later in a 3-1 defeat. Best then hit a dry spell in front of goal, by failing to hit the target in United's next eleven matches. During this run the Reds suffered an early exit from the League Cup at the hands of Blackpool with a 5-1 loss, however their league form kept them in contention for a good finish in Division One. The Belfast Boy rediscovered his scoring touch in November with a goal in a 3-1 away victory against Chelsea, where once again the right-back McCreadie was left looking foolish, after Best played a swift one-two around the defender with Sadler, before striking home the return pass. This result started a run of five wins on the spin which put them in pole position in Division One at the end of the month. Best added another goal to his tally on this run in a 2-1 victory over Leicester City at Filbert Street before netting two goals against local rivals Liverpool at Old Trafford on December 10th 1966. George played the first part of the season predominantly wearing the number 11 shirt, however, he reverted back to his more productive number seven shirt on 26th November 1966 and played on the outside right for the remainder of the season in all but one of United's league games.

After a 2-1 Boxing Day defeat away to Sheffield United, Matt Busby's men then went on a 20 game unbeaten run in the league. During the latter stages of the season, Best's goals became vital towards United's title quest and on 27th March 1967 his early strike against Fulham helped United towards a well fought 2-2 draw at

Craven Cottage. Five days later the Reds then beat West Ham 3-0 at Old Trafford with Best scoring United's second four minutes from the end. Then with three games to go, the United number seven sealed a 3-1 home victory over Aston Villa with United's third goal after the visitors had taken an early lead. The Reds were now within touching distance of a second league title in three years, knowing that victory in their penultimate game against West Ham at Upton Park would confirm them as champions. On May 6th 1967 United were indeed crowned as the division's elite, after thrashing the Londoners 6-1 on their own patch. George Best scored United's fourth goal in the rout after only 25 minutes when he flicked the ball from right to left before whacking it past a dishevelled Mackleworth in the Hammer's goal. Best had now been part of a title winning team for the second time; and at the tender age of 20, he now had his sights set on conquering Europe as United qualified for the prestigious competition as champions of England for the second time since the Munich Air Disaster.

Best in Europe: Best in Europe

United lost their first match of the 1967/1968 season 3-1 to Everton at Goodison Park, yet they remained unbeaten in their next 13 games in all competitions. Best's first goals of the season came during this sequence, when he scored a late equaliser against Sheffield Wednesday on September 16th 1967 before netting a brace against Tottenham Hotspur at Old Trafford the following week. Either side of the Spurs match, United overcame Hiberians Malta over two legs by winning 4-0 at Old Trafford, before playing out a goalless draw in the Mediterranean at the Empire Stadium. The Reds then won their next four matches, with Best scoring in the last game of this run in a 4-0 win at home to Coventry City. The United number seven was on the score sheet again three days later, however his 71st minute strike against Nottingham Forest at the City Ground came in a 3-1 defeat.

George then reverted to the number 10 shirt for the following seven matches, playing in a more central position in the absence of Denis Law who was suffering from an injury-hit campaign. The Northern Irishman scored four goals in this period, with two goals coming at Anfield in a 2-1 win over Liverpool on November 11th 1967 before netting another double against West Bromwich Albion three weeks later at Old Trafford.

These two results came either side of a two-legged tie in the European Cup, where Manchester United faced the champions of Yugoslavia, FK Sarajevo on November 29th 1967. After drawing 0-0 in the first leg at the Stadion Kosevo, United took part in In a scrappy, stop-start affair at Old Trafford with the referee penalising all kinds of fouls. United took the lead after 10 minutes when Aston poached the ball home at the far post. Once behind, the visiting players became more vitriolic in their tackling, especially towards the United danger man George Best. This did not deter the United forward as early in the second half Best collected an Alex Stepney throw, then ran from half way, skinning the Sarajevo defence before his deflected shot hit the post and bounced away to safety. The antics from the Yugoslavians started to rile the home side, particularly George Best who appeared to lash out Goalkeeper Muftic after the Sarajevo number one had helped the youngster off his feet with excessive force. With Muftic holding his face, the away side decided to take matters into their own hands when Fahrudin Prljasea brutally chopped down George Best on the edge of the box which resulted in the referee sending the Sarajevo player off the field.

Best got his revenge when the following free-kick was headed onto the bar by Bill Foulkes, before Francis Burns hooked the ball back into the area, where the Belfast Boy smashed home a volley on 63 minutes. It was the ultimate display of Best's character and epitomised him as a man, as he got up from being savagely kicked from the visiting defenders to score the crucial second goal. Sarajevo pulled one back which emphasized the importance of Best's goal, as that strike proved to be the winner. Any other player may have shirked the opportunity to score under the circumstances, and if George Best did not have the audacity to get up and shoot then Manchester United may have gone out of the European Cup.

From Boxing Day where Best scored two goals against Wolverhampton Wanderers in a 4-0 win at Old Trafford, the United talisman went through a goalscoring purple patch where he netted 9 goals in 9 games. After scoring in consecutive home games against

West Ham United in a 3-1 win, before netting a brace against Sheffield Wednesday in a 4-2 victory, the Reds then hosted Tottenham in the F.A. Cup third round. George cancelled out Spurs' early goal when he jinked his way past the visitor's defence to score after 4 minutes. However, the away side equalised in the last minute after Charlton put United ahead in the second half. The replay saw Matt Busby's men eliminated from the F.A. Cup at the first hurdle, however, their league form remained consistent throughout the new year. Best netted a goal apiece in his next two games with a revenge 2-1 victory away to Tottenham in the league before opening the scoring against Burnley at Turf Moor in a 2-1 defeat.

If it was possible for defenders to fear the genius of George Best anymore, his hot streak in front of goal appeared to amplify this fear when United faced Arsenal on February 24th 1968. After 23 minutes, Alex Stepney launched the ball forward towards into the Arsenal half, which was chased down by George Best and Arsenal's Peter Storey, who's job in this match was to mark the United forward. As the ball neared the touchline, it was somehow diverted unfathomably into the Arsenal goal to give Manchester United the lead. On closer inspection it appeared that Storey, who was panicked by the presence of Best, tried to pass the ball back to to his goalkeeper Jim Furnell, however, the Gunner's 'keeper was caught off guard and the ball landed in his net. Many reports suggested that George Best was now so good that he could score without even touching the ball. He did, however, officially get on the score sheet on 56 minutes when Law headed down a Kidd cross into the path of the Northern Irishman. It appeared that there was no path to goal for Best as he twisted and turned in the Arsenal half. However, with one jolt of the hip he managed to create an opening which saw him venture forward, before rifling the ball into the top corner of the net from the edge of the box.

United's next match was against Polish champions Gornik Zabrze at Old Trafford in the quarter-final of the European Cup, where Best helped to break the deadlock after his cross was diverted into his own net by Gornik's Stefan Florenski. The game ended 2-0 after Kidd added a second. A 1-0 defeat in Poland saw United scrape through on aggregate meaning they gained a place in the semi-finals and came one step closer to achieving Sir Matt Busby's life-long dream.

One of George Best's most important attributes was his nervelessness for the big occasion. Prior to the quarter-final against Gornik, the Belfast Boy was seen drinking a cup of tea outside the ground less than 30 minutes before the kick-off with his friend Mike Summerbee, before he rushed off to get changed. This unwavering persona from Best did not have an effect on how he started the game, as any suggestion of ill-preparation was blown out of the water when he scored inside the first minute in the Manchester Derby on March 27th 1968 at Old Trafford, after he slotted the ball past City Goalkeeper Ken Mulhearn with consummate ease. Although United went on to lose the Derby match 3-1 he then repeated his heroics in United's next match three days later against Stoke City at the Victoria Ground, when he opened the scoring after only 2 minutes in a 4-2 victory for the Reds. The following week United played Liverpool at Old Trafford and barely a minuted had been played when the United winger, with the number seven emblazoned on his back, broke free. After Charlton put him through on goal, following a poor free-kick from Liverpool's Ron Yeats, the in-form Best then rifled the ball past the visiting goalkeeper Tommy Lawrence to score his 20th league goal of the season. This match did, however, end up in a 2-1 defeat for the Reds, yet it was evident that George Best's ulterior pass-times were having little effect in hampering his performances. It was if the Belfast Boy was trying to score straight from the kick-off to prove a point.

United had now lost four games in six matches which put a massive dent in their title-winning ambitions, yet Best's goalscoring run continued with a double first-half strike away to Fulham in a 4-0 win on April 12th 1968 before netting the equaliser against Southampton in a 2-2 draw at the Dell the following day. The reverse fixture two days later against Fulham at Old Trafford saw Best score again, which meant United's leading scorer had notched-up 7 goals in 6 games. Now everyone's attention turned towards the biggest match in United's history so far – a European Cup semi-final encounter against the mighty Real Madrid.

On April 24th 1968 United kicked-off the first leg of their semi-final at Old Trafford. A weight of expectancy was on the home side as the reigning champions of England looked to gain a decent lead before heading to the cauldron of the Bernabeu Stadium. The first half was a stalemate as United failed to capitalise on a number of chances, yet ten minutes into the second half Johnny Aston weaved his way through the right hand side of the Real defence, before cutting it back for George Best, who swept the ball ferociously into the top corner of the net. It was another momentous occasion for Best who seemed to be the calmest man in the ground on a night of extreme nervous tension. This goal proved to be the only goal of the game, which gave United a slender advantage before travelling to the Spanish capital. Best's contribution was even more admirable as he admitted after the match that an ankle injury had been niggling him for weeks. It prevailed to be a night that would be remembered for his lion-heartedness rather than the skill of a genius, yet George was now recognised as a player who had the capability of showing both in abundance.

Before the second leg of this tie United had to play three remaining league fixtures with the Division One title still hanging in the balance, as they vied with neighbours Manchester City and Liverpool for the top spot. A 6-3 defeat to West Brom at the Hawthorns saw United lose the initiative in the run-in, then the penultimate game of the season came against Newcastle at Old Trafford, which was now a must win game for the Reds. The players rose to the occasion as Kidd opened the scoring inside ten minutes, before George Best made his mark on the game. Mid-way through the first half, Best added another peach of a goal to his season's tally with an eighteen-yard drive after Crerand nodded a Charlton corner into his path. Best then made it 3-0 before half-time with a well-executed penalty. Another spot-kick from the United number seven earned him the first hat-trick of his career, and also his 30th goal of the season, before the home side added two more goals to win 6-0. United needed to win the last game of the season against Sunderland and hope that other results went their way, if they were to retain the Division One crown. After 33 minutes at Old Trafford, however, Sunderland found themselves two goals to the good. George Best did grab a consolation goal just before half-time with arguably his best long-range effort of the season. After a bout of head tennis between the two teams, the ball bounced kindly for best, who steadied himself before unleashing a rasping volley with the outside of his right-foot, which arced into the bottom corner of the Sunderland net.

United finished the campaign in second place behind their neighbours Manchester City, yet their season was not over, as finishing top of the pile in Europe now became their priority.

On May 15th 1968 Manchester United faced Real Madrid in the second leg of the European Cup semi-final at the Bernabeu Stadium. As the first half played-out, The 1-0 lead that Matt Busby's men took with them from the first leg started to look futile. Soon the Spanish champions turned on the style, flipping the tie on its head by giving themselves a two goal lead after 41 minutes. United pulled one back through a Zoco own goal two minutes later, however, the home side immediately restored their lead to give themselves a 3-1 advantage at the break. Although all seemed lost, the Reds only needed one goal to level the game as a whole, which gave them an added incentive going into the second half. Then after 75 minutes United grabbed a goal back after Best's flick header gave Sadler the opportunity to find the net to make the score 3-2 on the night and 3-3 on aggregate.

To get a result at the Bernabeu at the best of times was a tall order, while being 3-1 behind at half time usually did not give visiting teams a prayer. Yet somehow Manchester United were playing for a cause greater than the game on the night and greater than football itself. They had a manager and playing staff who had set out to conquer Europe ten years earlier that were still at the club. They were the same men who watched their teammates and friends perish around them, trying achieve the same ambition that they had burning on this night in Spain. It was the swinging hips of Best which provided United with their next opportunity, as he weaved his way down the right wing with a determined purpose. He then cut back a cross which was diverted into the goal. Inexplicably, it was centre-half Bill Foulkes who found the net on this occasion to level the scores on the night. The same man who survived the Munich Air Disaster ten years previous abandoned his post in searched of an equaliser.

Manchester United had collectively risked and lost so much in their pursuit of European glory that Bill Foulkes realised they had nothing more to lose. The big defender who was a primary source from the swaggering Busby Babe's European escapades had now gambled with a now or never venture forward; and it was Best who was the provider. It paid off and Manchester United won thanks to two assists from George Best and a game played with a steely-hearted sentiment.

Manchester United now faced Benfica at Wembley in the European Cup final in the biggest night of their lives. This would be the first time the two teams teams had met since George Best was dubbed 'El Beatle' two years earlier, after his age-defying performance at the Estadio da Luz.

Benfica looked better equipped to deal with George and United this time around, however, their use of underhand tactics and persistent fouling on the Belfast Boy clearly stated that their intentions were to stop him from playing. Benfica's Fernando Cruz appeared to have been given the orders to do a job on Best, prompting the United forward to switch sides in an attempt to gain more freedom. The Portuguese side initially managed to nullify United and the first real chance came from Eusabio who hit the bar with a long-range attempt early in the game. Despite being kicked from pillar to post, George continued to make things happen, before Benfica's Humberto was cautioned by the referee for one too many fouls on a clearly fired-up Best. A disallowed goal from the Northern Irishman was perhaps a warning shot, before he continued to dance his way around the Wembley stage.

On 53 minutes the deadlock was broken by Bobby Charlton, who headed home a David Sadler cross to give United the lead. Best then set on another one of his mesmeric slalom rides through the Benfica defence before seeing his shot parried by the opposing goalkeeper Jose Henrique, with Sadler's follow-up being stopped by the Benfica number one once again. Best continued to be the biggest threat posed to the Portuguese opposition, however, his marauds towards goal failed to produce the desired result. Benfica then equalised with ten minutes remaining through Graca, which silenced the overwhelming support that United had brought with them to the capital. Soon their was an air of fear looming around the summer air of London as United began to leave gaps at the back. With three minutes remaining, the European Cup appeared to be lost as Jose Augusto set the irrepressible Eusabio through on goal. With the Portuguese forward bearing down on the United goal and with the whites of Alex Stepney's eyes beginning to emerge in his hair-pin eye-sight, Eusabio unleashed a shot with such a ferocious trajectile that there seemed to be no other outcome other than the net to bulge. Somehow the United number one not only saved the attempt on goal, he managed to cling onto it, prompting the Benfica number ten to personally congratulate Stepney on his heroic intervention. The game then went to extra-time and with tired limbs and tired minds it seemed that United had to find something from somewhere. Then two minutes into the additional thirty, Stepney launched a long clearance up the field, where Brian Kidd headed the ball forwards into the path of George Best.

A piece of magic or a flash of brilliance was needed. Anything that would bring home the trophy which Manchester United pioneered for England in its infancy. To make the vision of Sir Matt Busby become a reality, to justify the efforts of everyone associated with Manchester United who had obsessively pursued the Holy Grail of Europe with great abandon and sacrifice. For a momentary reprieve for the loss and heartache of Taylor, Pegg, Whelan, Jones, Byrne, Coleman, Bent and Edwards. To become the first English team to win the trophy.

Best's next move was to flick the ball through the legs of Benfica defender Jacinto Santos before he strode towards the goal. With Jose Henrique the only barrier between him and the goal, every Manchester United fan inside the ground and watching at home were mentally kicking the ball into the net. However Best decided to round the goalkeeper with a swagger that only the Belfast Boy could produce. This was George Best personified. On the biggest stage and in the biggest match in club football, the Northern Irishman, who had been fouled since the get-go, still had the bravery and audacity to continue playing the way he only knew. He never seemed rushed or panicked. The occasion did not phase him, he did it his way and in his own time. With the floodlit number seven on his shirt ruffling in the London night air, the moment of iconography had been captured. The man who was named the Football Writer's Player of the Year became the man of the moment. As the audiences in every destination, including the goalkeeper, leant to the right, George Best had already gone left. He then calmly passed the ball between the goal posts and turned away before he even saw the net move, which was where both the ball and the goalkeeper ended up buried. This knocked the wind out of

Benfica's sails and with two further goals from Kidd and Charlton, United already had the game wrapped up in the first period of extra-time with a 4-1 score-line.

So United were crowned champions of Europe for the first time and it was George Best's guile and impudence which opened the extra-time floodgates. He scored 32 goals that season in all competitions, with the last of those being the most important of his career so far. With George turning 22 just a few days before the final, it seemed that there would be plenty more to come from the young forward. Yet the images of Best in his number seven shirt from that day at Wembley would be hard to topple. The Northern Irishman was now a recognised superstar and his life would probably never be the same. As for the shirt, it seemed evident that the number seven jersey was now no longer an ordinary piece of football kit.

Manchester United started the 1968/69 season where they left off with a 2-1 win over Everton at Old Trafford with Best netting the opening goal. Yet the hangover from the previous European Cup winning season soon kicked in with United only winning 2 of their next 8 league games, with Best notching only one goal in this sequence in a 5-4 defeat to Sheffield Wednesday at Hillsborough at the end of August. United ended this poor run of league form with a 3-1 win over Newcastle at Old Trafford with George scoring two goals, yet the attention of the side now turned to the World Club Championship against Estudiantes.

The first leg turned out to be a physical affair against the South American Champions, who brought gamesmanship and foul play to a new level. Many opposing teams had singled out George in the past for special treatment on the field, yet this time not one United player escaped the win-at-all-costs brutality of the Argentinian team. Before Best was floored with a punch by Carlos Pachame, Nobby Stiles and Bobby Charlton required treatment for cuts and gashes coming from fouls by the home side. Stiles eventually received a frivolous sending-off for two bookings. The first for standing to close to an Estudiantes player, then for raising an arm in protest at an offside decision. United lost the game 1-0, however, they were undoubtedly relieved to get through the match without a serious injury.

The second leg at Old Trafford on 16th October 1968 was once again a tempestuous affair and a frustrating one for the Reds, as they struggled to make inroads into the visitors defence. Then a few minutes from time, the game started to boil over. After Best attempted a cross into the Estudiantes box, Jose Medina caught the United forward with a late tackle. George, who had resisted rising to the bait throughout the two legs, suddenly threw a punch at the Argentinian defender, who then threw himself to the ground histrionically. The incident subsequently led to both players receiving their marching orders - the first sending-off of George Best's career. United did pull a goal back through Morgan, yet it was the champions of South America who became the champions of the world. Best had endured the rough-house approach from defenders, both domestically and in Europe for many years. He seldom retaliated in a violent way, instead his preferred retort was to make his opponents look silly with his skill and flair on the pitch. However, this appeared to be one antagonistic action too far for the Belfast Boy, who may well have finally snapped after years of suffering defenders using underhand tactics to stop him. Yet others believed there may have been a rebellious streak in George that extended beyond the parameters of the football field.

Either side of the first leg United overcame Irish Minnows Waterford in the European Cup first leg, with a 3-1 win at Lansdowne Road, before dishing out a 7-1 thrashing at Old Trafford. Despite this the Reds continued to perform poorly in Division One, with only one win in nine league games following the Waterford match. In this run of games, Best scored in a 2-1 defeat to Southampton at Old Trafford on 26th October 1968 before netting two goals in a 3-2 win at Queen Park Rangers a week later. After United won 4-3 on aggregate over two legs against Anderlecht, a game which Best missed through suspension, he then made his final goalscoring contribution of the calendar year, by netting just before the hour mark at home to Wolves in 2-0 win.

It was this year that George Best picked up the European Player of the Year award. Since the final against Benfica back in May, Best became a global superstar and at the age of only 22, he still had many years ahead of him to accomplish great things. However, on January 14th 1969, the newly knighted Sir Matt Busby announced that he would be retiring from his post as the Manchester United manager at the end of the season. The man that had nurtured Best's prodigious talent since he was in his early teens was now leaving the monumental task of managing George and Manchester United to someone else.

The Reds still had the rest of the season with Sir Matt at the helm and United responded with a 4-1 win on January 18th 1969 against Sunderland at Old Trafford, where Best scored United's fourth goal. The Northern Irish international then scored the equaliser in a 2-2 draw with Wolves at Molineux four weeks later. Either side of this match United faced Birmingham City in the F.A. Cup fifth round. United progressed through the first two rounds at the expense of Exeter City in a 3-1 away win and a 2-0 replayed win over Watford at Vicarage Road. The Birmingham match also appeared to be heading for a replay when the score was locked at 1-1 with time running out. Yet eight minutes from the end, Charlton crossed a dangerous ball into the box towards Best, who spun gracefully before slamming the ball home. United thought they had the game in the bag, yet three minutes later Best handled the ball in his own area causing the referee to point to the penalty spot. Birmingham converted the spot-kick forcing the game into a replay at Old Trafford. United did not make the same mistake this time round as they dished out a 6-2 hammering over the Midland team. George did not score in this match, however, he was instrumental in this riveting performance, causing havoc whenever he was on the ball. At one point in the match, Best bobbed and weaved through five opposing defenders before seeing his shot hit the post. It was evident that George was still living up to the tag of being the number one player in Europe, moreover, Manchester United looked back to their goalscoring best.

United's next match was against Austrian champions Rapid Vienna at Old Trafford in the first leg of the European Cup quarter-final. It was George Best who broke the deadlock in this match when he swivelled to score after Morgan's cut-back. After Morgan scored United's second, the Belfast Boy received a returned, chipped pass from Stiles, before he went to maraud the Vienna penalty area. After jigging, feinting and tip-toeing, Best placed the ball into the roof of the visitors goal. George spurned the opportunity to shoot until he made the last defender surrender. His feet were like fingers on a piano playing a melodious symphony, appropriately saving one of his best concertos for the team from the home of Mozart. He he was the boy with a rock star image, yet his movement was sometimes classical.

United progressed to the semi-finals as a result of a goalless draw in Vienna, yet in between these two legs the Reds were eliminated from the F.A. Cup quarter-final by Everton. Their attention then shifted to the league were they were languishing in the bottom half of the table. With no chance of mounting a title challenge, the Red's only chance of silverware was the European Cup, where A.C. Milan awaited them in the semi-finals.

Their below-par Division One form continued as United failed to win any of their next three games. Then on March 19th 1969 United faced Queens Park Rangers in a league match at Old Trafford. After Morgan had opened the scoring early on, Best then doubled United's lead just after half-time. After Kidd had slid a pass to Best, he then stopped the ball with his foot and waited to see if any Rangers player would be brave enough to challenge him. As two reluctant men stepped forward, Best dragged the ball away from them and fired the ball instantly into the corner of the net. The cheek of the goal even impressed the official, as he gave Best a congratulatory tap on the back when he walked back to the centre circle. Best then added another goal when he rounded three startled defenders, before rifling the ball home past a bewildered Spratley in the Q.P.R. Goal. United then added another 5 goals in the last 15 minutes as the rout ended 8-1 to the home side. The Reds had found their lethal touch again in front of goal, showing flashes of why they were the reigning champions of Europe, with Best duly receiving all the plaudits. Three days later, George scored the winner against Sheffield Wednesday in a 1-0 home win; interestingly he was wearing the number 9 shirt for the first time in his career in place of the injured Charlton.

At the end of March, Best started a run of four goals in three games with a winning penalty against Nottingham Forest at the City Ground, then a brace against West Bromwich Albion at Old Trafford, before netting his 20th goal of the season in the reverse fixture against Forest in a 3-1 win. In the penultimate league game of the season the Irishman added another goal to his tally in a 2-0 home win over Burnley, before notching a season's total of 22 goals with a last-day strike at Old Trafford, in a 3-2 win over Leicester City. In between these two matches United played their two-legged semi-final against A.C. Milan in the European Cup, where the the hopes of retaining the trophy were dented with a 2-0 first leg defeat at the San Siro. Although United did win the second leg at Old Trafford 1-0, it was not enough to send them through, meaning there would be no fairytale ending for the retiring Sir Matt Busby, who would now move upstairs.

The Flaws of a Genius

The 1969/70 season started badly for new coach Wilf McGuinness, as United failed to win any of their first six matches. Best helped United get back to winning ways with a goal in a 3-1 win over Sunderland at Old Trafford. Then a week later on September 6th 1969 Best netted twice against Leeds United in a 2-2 draw at Elland Road. His first came after he converted an Alan Gowling attempt on goal from the centre of the box. He then scored a screamer when he latched on to a Charlton pass, before lashing the ball in off the post from 20 yards, to give United a momentary lead.

United then found a run of form which was spearheaded by Best, starting with a 3-1 win over Sheffield Wednesday on September 17th 1969 when he scored two goals in two minutes at Hillsbrough. With the game tied at 1-1, Best rifled the ball home from close range to put the away side in the lead, before a pass from Charlton prompted Best to drive home United's third from the edge of the box. The Northern Irishman then netted another goal three days later at Highbury in a 2-2 draw with Arsenal. After being 2-0 down, Best pulled one back for the visitors after his angled shot went straight through the arms of Malcolm Webster just before half-time. He then created the second, after a majestic run through the opposing defence ended in Sadler poaching the ball off George's toe to equalise.

Following a mid-week League Cup goal against Wrexham at home, Best then helped United dismantle West Ham 5-2 at Old Trafford on September 27th 1969, by notching-up another two goals. Francis Burns opened the scoring for the Reds, before a Best header from a Morgan cross to put United 2-0 in front. Then after a Charlton goal and a double strike from West Ham's Geoff Hurst, Best netted another header, this time from an Aston cut-back. The in-form talisman then set-up Kidd for United's fifth goal after a mazy run inside the box.

After a defeat to Derby County the following week, Best then scored in three consecutive league matches at the start of October, starting with a goal against Southampton in a 3-0 win at the Dell. He then netted the first goal in a 2-1 home win over Ipswich, before scoring the equalising goal against Nottingham Forest at Old Trafford in a 1-1 draw. George then concluded a mesmeric, exhibition-like sequence of 13 goals in 13 games with the winner in the League Cup fourth round replay against Burnley at Old Trafford.

With the departure of the long-serving legendary manager and the general age and decline of the team, there seemed to be an over-reliance on Best, who was still only 23. The Belfast Boy was the main attraction for the thousands of fans piling through the turnstiles at football grounds across the country and still the best player in Europe. The fact that United were no longer in European competition only gave Best the domestic platform to demonstrate his unrivalled talent. It was apparent at this point that frustration started to creep into his game.

The Irishman then went through a barren spell by scoring only 1 goal in 12 games, with his only strike coming in the Division One match against Burnley at Turf Moor, in a 1-1 draw at the end of November. Despite this, United overcame Derby County via a replay, with a 1-0 win in the League Cup quarter-final at Old Trafford, meaning they faced a two-legged tie with Manchester City in the semi-final. The Reds lost the first leg at Maine Road 2-1 by the means of a late Francis Lee penalty. They then failed to make amends in the second leg at Old Trafford after a 2-2 draw, which contained more controversy as Mike Summerbee converted the rebound off an indirect free-kick which was allowed to stand, as United goalkeeper Stepney handled the initial shot. Best's Moment of Genius in this match came when a 50 yard run, which split the whole visiting team apart, ended in Denis Law giving United a momentary lead in the tie; however, a moment of madness at the end of the first leg cost George his place in United side. After the final whistle in the first leg, Best displayed more of his tempestuousness when he hit the ball out of referee Jack Taylor's hands, seemingly in protest at the late penalty which was awarded to the home side. This lead to a £100 fine and a one month suspension. The ban started three games after the semi-final, where United managed to remain unbeaten until George returned to action against Northampton Town in the F.A. Cup 5th round on February 7th 1970.

United had overcome Ipswich 1-0 in the third round, which was Best's last game before the ban, then in his absence they acted revenge on neighbours Manchester City in a 3-0 win at Old Trafford in round four. After five weeks without any competitive match practice, it seemed the Northern Irishman may need a few games under his belt to get back into his stride. Yet George Best was a player who defied footballing logic, he was a man who played with complete abandonment despite the circumstances. In any given match and on any given occasion, the United forward could produce the spectacular. He was not a player who had to work hard for his talent, by now it was evident that he was a natural born genius.

Best wasted no time in making an impact upon his return to first team football, as he opened the scoring with a far post header after a searching ball from Kidd. Then only a minute later he doubled United's lead after latching on to a Crerand pass, before rounding the goalkeeper and sliding the ball home. Best continued to tantalise the Northampton defence, with George seeing a barnstorming run-and-shot saved by Kim Book in the Cobbler's goal. He then netted his hat trick after another assist from Kidd, who's low centre was lashed into the roof of the net by the rampant Best, after his first effort was blocked. Best then scored his fourth goal of the game with a diving header from another Kidd cross, which nestled in the bottom corner of Book's goal. After Kidd scored United's fifth, the Belfast Boy then received a through-ball from Burns, before calmly placing the ball into the left of the Northampton net as he bared down on goal, to make it 6-0. Kidd then added another goal to the rout before Northampton pulled one back to make the scoreline 7-1. Then towards the end Crerand teed-up Best, who danced past the last defender on the edge of the box, floored the goal keeper with another jink of his legs and then cheekily slotted the ball home in the opposite corner with his left foot. The cup tie ended 8-2 and the former European Player of the Year had now set a new goal-scoring record for Manchester United with 6 goals in one game.

In one match George Best scored two with head, three with his right foot and one with his left foot. It was the perfect double hat trick, it was the exhibition of an artist, a repertoire of a genius. It was the perfect repost from Best who's reputation had been muddied by the F.A. worse than the mud clad pitch in Northampton. He, like many, felt the punishment did not fit the crime and it was believed that the harsh penalty initially only happened due to the profile of the player and the profile of the match. However, Best found his own liberty on that day at the County Ground.

George Best's next goal came in a 3-3 thriller against Burnley at Old Trafford on March 17th 1970. After United had trailed 3-1, Law pulled a goal back before Best equalised with only two minutes left on the clock. Then more controversy surrounded Best whilst on international duty. After disagreeing with a referee's decision in an international match between Northern Ireland and Scotland, Best appeared to throw mud at the official in protest. This act of petulance led to the Northern Irishman being sent-off by the referee involved in the incident. George's rebellion and the air of freedom in which he played the game, helped him produce moments with the ball that no-one else could dream of. However the common genius trait of going against the grain sometimes spilled over into off-the-ball situations. Sometimes the line between breaking the laws of nature with his prodigious talent and breaking the rules of the game became distorted. Hence he sometimes found it hard to deal with authority figures who deemed to be shackling his free-spirited nature. Together with the fact that Manchester United were clearly not the team they once were only encouraged this frustration to boil over.

Domestically Best was having a quiet end to the season scoring only 1 goal in a run of 13 games. An F.A. Cup semi-final defeat in a second replay to Leeds United confounded the misery at Old Trafford. Best did help to give the home fans something to shout about with three games to go when he netted the final goal in a 7-0 hammering of West Bromwich Albion. Then on the last game of the season the enigmatic Irishman opened the scoring for United in a 2-2 draw at Old Trafford against Sheffield Wednesday.

Despite the controversy that seemed to follow Best this season, the forward netted a total of 21 goals in 53 appearances, meaning the Northern Irishman had scored the most league goals for United for the third consecutive season.

The 1970/71 season started poorly for the Reds with only one win in their first five league games. George Best opened his account for the season six games in with the second goal in a 2-0 win over Everton at Old Trafford. After scoring in the League Cup first round against Aldershot in a 3-1 win at the Recreation Ground, he then netted another goals three days later in a 2-0 home win over Coventry City. Two weeks later on September 26th 1970 Manchester United faced Blackpool at Old Trafford where Best took his impudence to a new height. After good work from Morgan on the right, his cross arrowed towards George with a line of defenders in front of him and seemingly no space to shoot. Yet Best flicked the ball through his legs with a cheeky back heel that nestled in the bottom corner of the net. Perhaps George thought his ever growing repertoire was missing a back-heeled goal.

United then overcame Portsmouth in round three of the League Cup, however, Best went through a temporary lean spell in the league as he chalked-up eight Division One matches without a goal. Amidst this run, United's attention turned back to the League Cup and on October 28th 1970, when Manchester United played Chelsea in the fourth round of the competition, George Best took dribbling into a new art form. In a 2-1 win at Old Trafford, George Best was put clear on goal with defenders closing in on him like spiked walls in a horror film. One of these defenders was the notorious hatchet-man Ron 'Chopper' Harris who flew in from the side and whacked the United forward with his studs high. Somehow, Best stayed on his feet without even flinching, before rounding the goalkeeper and nonchalantly passing the ball into the net with two defenders still on the goal line. When the Northern Irishman had the ball at his feet he seemed to be able to put a hex on the ball, making it an orb of sorcery which was under his control. Yet when he was clattered by the brutish centre-halves of his era, it never seemed to break his stride. It was an athletic phenomenon how the youngster could stay on his feet after such collisions. It was difficult to tackle him, kicking him did not seem to work and there was not many that could catch him. Even to the best players of his era, he was the one player who seemed unstoppable.

At the end of November Best rediscovered his goalscoring touch in the league when he notched a goal in a 1-1 draw with Huddersfield at Old Trafford. Then in United's next match on December 5th 1970 against Tottenham Hotspur at White Hart Lane, the United forward netted another when he sublimely chested down a John Fitzpatrick cross, before caressing the ball into the bottom corner of Pat Jennings' goal.

United were then eliminated from the League Cup at the semi-final stage over two legs against Aston Villa, before the Reds took part in a thriller on a snow covered pitch at the Baseball ground on Boxing Day against Derby County, where George scored United's second goal in a 4-4 draw.

After this result Wilf McGuinness was sacked as Manchester United's manager, meaning Sir Matt Busby would take over for the remainder of the season. This coincided with Best attending an F.A. Disciplinary meeting regarding his behaviour, due to the fact he received three cautions for misconduct in twelve months. He allegedly arrived three hours late, before receiving a £250 fine and a six week suspended sentence. The next day George defiantly scored a consolation goal against Middlesbrough, in a 2-1 defeat in the F.A. Cup 3rd Round. Three days later Best missed the train to London for United's league match with Chelsea, prompting Sir Matt to suspend George for two weeks.

Despite the unruly Irishman having momentary lapses of timekeeping, George Best's ability to beat any defensive cordon was never in doubt at this stage; and his goalscoring was always synonymous with weaving and jinking past his opponents to find the net. However, on February 6th 1971 in a league match against Tottenham Hotspur at Old Trafford, he found another way to beat four defenders and a goalkeeper. As Paddy Crerand chipped a pass into the box, the ball broke free to Best twelve yards from goal, yet there was too many defenders clogging up the goal mouth for him to see even a snippet of the net. Best, who was wearing number eleven that day, impudently lobbed the ball from a seemingly impossible angle, over the Spurs defence and into the net. The Tottenham defence looked at each other in befuddlement, yet George Best had his arm aloft celebrating yet another inconceivable goal.

A top half finish in the league was now the best United could hope for considering their patchy form in the first half of the season. It was now that George Best turned on the magic for the Manchester fans, as he went on a blistering goalscoring streak, netting 11 goals in the final 12 games.

After scoring in a 4-3 loss away West Brom at the start of March, the Belfast Boy then scored the second goal in a 2-0 win over Nottingham Forest at Old Trafford. Then on March 20th 1971 in a 2-1 win, George opened the scoring against Stoke City at the Victoria Ground with another goal of the season contender. After 23 minutes Charlton lobbed the ball forward to Best, who bamboozled the last defender before crashing the ball home off the underside of the crossbar from the acutest of angles. He then added another goal which was vintage George Best. After nicking the ball off a Stoke defender on the edge of the box, who then fell in his wake, a twist of the hips then left the goalkeeper on the floor like a turtle on its back. Best then slid the ball into the net with another chasing defender lying face down in the goalmouth. At times George left the opposing penalty areas an utter maelstrom, with bodies strewn all over the place. Now with his mentor Sir Matt Busby back at the helm, it gave the Irishman more of an incentive to create havoc on the pitch, rather than off it.

Best's next two goals came in consecutive 2-1 away losses to West Ham and then Coventry City. United then Travelled to Selhurst Park on April 17th 1971 where they found themselves 2-0 down inside 24 minutes. However, after two goals from Law either side of half time United drew themselves level. Then Best got himself in on the act mid-way through the second half, as the man who was back in his iconic number seven shirt, volleyed the ball into the net from inside the box to give United the lead.

The Northern Irishman then extended United's advantage after he won the ball on the halfway line, then flicked it to Crerand who's return pass was rocketed so ferociously towards goal by Best that the Palace keeper simply could not hold on to the ball as it found its way into the net. Law then completed his hat trick before Palace nicked a goal back as the game ended 5-3 to the Reds. The following week, a first half George Best penalty helped United to a 3-2 win over Ipswich

Town at Old Trafford, then United ended the season on a high with a Derby win over Manchester City at Maine Road. The Reds stormed into a 3-0 first half lead with the Holy Trinity of Charlton, Law and Best fittingly scoring the goals in Sir Matt Busby's final game as Manchester United manager. City pulled one back before Best then scored the final goal of Sir Matt's reign to make it 4-1. The home side scored two goals towards the end produce a nervy finish for United, however the Reds held on to win 4-3.

Despite an unsettling period for George at the turn of the year, the Belfast Boy still managed to return to his dazzling best during the second part of the campaign. He netted 21 goals in 48 matches for United this term, whilst top scoring in the league for the fourth consecutive season.

United finished eighth in Division One for the second year running and it would be fair to say that without George Best during the last three years, United could have been in serious trouble. Sometimes the price of a Genius is worth paying in terms of tolerating George's antics away from the game, because of what he could produce in it. However, this conundrum would be up to new manager Frank O'Farrell to solve, as he would now be the man responsible for reigning the Northern Irish froward in.

United started the 1971/72 campaign in a cloud of controversy of their own when they were forced to play their first two home matches on neutral grounds. This was following an incident in the previous season, where a knife had allegedly been thrown from the stands in a league match at Old Trafford against Newcastle United. Despite this United started the season well and remained unbeaten in heir first five games by winning three and drawing two. However, not being one to shun the limelight, Best was sent-off in United's second game of the season against Chelsea just before half-time, after the home team had scored. His marching orders were given for being demonstrative to the referee after Morgan had been booked for dissent. United did however recover to win the match 3-2. Yet even with a suspended sentence hanging over his head, Best was eventually cleared of dissent by the Football Association after it was unclear whether his tirade was aimed at the referee or teammate Willie Morgan.

After United beat Arsenal 3-1 in their first 'home' game of the season at Anfield, they then hosted West Bromwich Albion at Stoke's Victoria Ground in the second game of their Old Trafford ban where they won 3-1 again, with Best scoring two goals. The next game saw Best open the scoring in a 1-1 draw with Wolverhampton Wanders at Molineux, before notching his fourth goal of the season in United's first game at Old Trafford since the ban, with a winner against Ipswich Town. Three days later Best was the bane of Ipswich again, this time in round 2 of the League Cup where the Irishman netted two goals in a 3-1 win at Portman Road. Having been cleared by the F.A. of any misconduct and with United flying high near the top of Division One, it appeared that George Best had now found inner peace as a Manchester United footballer.

On September 18th 1971 Manchester United hosted West Ham United at Old Trafford where the Reds looked to continue their impressive league form. It was Best who led the charge in this match and after an early long-ranger from George was tipped onto the bar by Bobby Ferguson in the Hammers' goal, he then nodded in the resulting corner at the far post. After West Ham equalised, Best then restored United's lead when another corner by the home side eventually bounced to the Irishman, who pivoted on one foot before performing a back-breaking volley the with the other foot, causing the ball to fly into the top corner of net from close range. The visitors then levelled the game once more, before Charlton made the score 3-2 mid-way through the second half. United made sure of the win when George Best received a short corner near the touchline and jinked his way into the United box. After turning West Ham's John McDowell inside out, he then ghosted sideways past the two centre-backs before rifling the ball past a helpless Ferguson, to secure the third hat trick of his career and a 4-2 victory for United.

Best appeared to be in the form of his life and after a 2-2 draw with Liverpool, United went on a four match winning streak in the league, with Best scoring in each of these games. His first was the opening goal in a 2-0 win over league leaders Sheffield United at Old Trafford, which started when he received the ball just inside the opposing half of the field. As Best took the ball forward he looked around for passing options, yet with no-one in a good position to receive the ball, Best just kept on running, beating the first two defenders for pace. As he approached the edge of the box another wall of white shirts stood in his way, forcing the Northern Irishman wide of the goal into a seemingly impossible shooting angle. Yet George, who was now at full pace and a yard in front of the last defender, somehow whipped the ball past Hope in the Blades' goal before it cannoned of the far post and into the net.

Even though it seemed that Best had already achieved the impossible enough times in his career, he went and did it again. As he galloped past the whole Sheffield United back line, with his magical sleight-of-foot tricks and his dark hair waving in the wind, the white shirts of the league's leaders waved in submission. It was a goal that nobody else in the country could score. It was a genius at work.

United then beat Huddersfield town 3-0 at Leeds Road in their next league match, where Best opened the scoring with a powerful, leaping header from a Morgan cross. The in-form forward then scored the winning goals in consecutive matches, the first coming against Derby County at Old Trafford in a 1-0 win. Then in the second half against Newcastle at St James' Park he netted the winner after poaching a rebounded effort from Kidd a few yards from goal, to put United top of the league with another 1-0 win.

At the end of October United lost their first match after going twelve games unbeaten since the end of August, when they suffered a 1-0 home defeat to Leeds United. However their good form continued as although they were eliminated from the League Cup after a 2-1 second replay defeat to Stoke City at the Victoria ground, they remained unbeaten in the league for the rest of the year. During this run, United travelled to the south coast to play Southampton on November 27th 1971. The Reds opened the scoring after a Kidd cross found the head of George Best who nodded home from close range. After Sammy McIlroy had doubled United's lead, Charlton then drove a splitting ball into the box to Best, who instantly brought the ball under his spell whilst simultaneously performing a body swerve which left his marker on his back. He then left the last defender discombobulated as a double-shuffle allowed him room to bury the ball in the Saint's goal. After the home side pulled one back, George then claimed his second hat trick of the season and the fourth of his career when a Willie Morgan ball was picked up by Best in the

Southampton box. He saw his first two efforts blocked, however, at the third attempt he impishly headed the ball from an awkward position to give United a 4-1 lead. Southampton added another before Kidd finished the scoring for the Reds giving United a 5-2 win at the Dell, confirming their place at the top of the league and maintaining their record of being the league's top scorers. Yet at the turn of the year United's season took a turn for the worst. After losing away to West Ham on New Year's Day, George Best did not show up for training the following week. Manager O'Farrell fined Best two weeks wages and ordered him to take part in extra training as punishment for his actions.

Although the situation seemed to be dealt with, the events in early January clearly had an effect on United's league form, as their Division One campaign capitulated after they started the year with seven straight league defeats. The Reds did find some temporary salvation in the F.A. Cup, where upon George Best's return to action the Belfast Boy netted two goals in a 4-1 replay win over Southampton at Old Trafford, after drawing the first match 1-1 at the Dell. United then progressed to the fifth round after a 2-0 win away to Preston North End, where the Reds beat Middlesbrough 3-0 in a replay at Ayresome Park, after a goalless draw at home, with Best scoring his 20th goal of the season in the North-East fixture.

United's first league win of the calendar year came against Huddersfield Town on March 11th 1972 at Old Trafford, where the enigmatic Best opened the scoring in a 2-0 victory. A week later he then scored a late equaliser in the F.A. Cup quarter-final against Stoke City at Old Trafford, when he lashed home a Morgan cross, before netting the opening goal in the replay at the Victoria Ground three days later, although United eventually lost the match 2-1 after extra time. Best then added another spectacular goal to his collection when he volleyed the ball home from 25 yards against Coventry City at Highfield Road in a 3-2 win. After four games without a win, United then restored some pride with a 3-2 home victory over Southampton, where George added another goal to his season's tally. On the eve of the next match against Nottingham Forest it was reported that the Irishman had again missed training, which made him unavailable for the league match at the City Ground which resulted in a goalless draw.

After a 3-0 away defeat to Arsenal in the next league match, the Reds then hosted Stoke City in the final game of the season On April 29th 1972, where Best scored from the penalty spot just before half time to wrap-up a 3-0 win for United.

The season ended with Manchester United finishing 8th in Division One for the third consecutive campaign. The first half of the season which promised so much, saw George at his sizzling best, having notched 16 goals before the end of November whilst firing United to the top of the league as the highest scorers in the Division. However, his prodigious talent which single-handedly catapulted Manchester United to the summit of English football at the end of the year, was neutralised in the second part of the campaign by his troubled soul, which is so often the burden carried by such phenomenons.

The Greatest Ever

In the summer of 1972 the national press alleged that George Best had decided to quit football altogether. However despite the rumours, Best decided to return to Old Trafford at the start of the season, a season which started horrifically for United as they failed to win any of their first 9 league games. During this run, Best netted an equalising penalty against Leicester City in a 1-1 draw at Old Trafford, then ten days later on September 2nd 1972 Best opened the scoring in a 2-2 draw away to West Ham, when he danced his way around Bryan 'Pop' Robson in the Hammer's midfield before striking the ball into the bottom corner from 25 yards. The Irishman then netted a brace against Oxford United in the League Cup 2nd Round in a 3-1 replay win after drawing the first encounter 2-2. A penalty against West Brom on October 7th 1972 helped United earn a precious point in their quest to lift themselves off the bottom of the table, before netting in a 2-2 draw with Leicester City at Filbert Street in early November. Then 3 wins in 4 games saw United ease the pressure on themselves at the foot of Division One. During this run, on October 28th 1972, the Holy Trinity of George Best, Denis Law and Bobby Charlton played together for the last time. Then a month later with United's dismal league form dominating the back pages, the press now had a field day with George Best's return to the front pages, after it was reported that the Northern Irishman had once again missed training. O'Farrell duly dropped Best for United's next match with Norwich City. Then on December 5th 1972 it was reported that George Best had been put on the transfer list.

However, three weeks later this was retracted as Best returned to training. Yet his return did not seem a welcome one, as many of his teammates and board members were now becoming disillusioned with the whole ordeal. Best was a law unto himself on the pitch, he did what whatever he wanted with the ball at his feet, yet because he could produce a moment of genius with his end-product, this was never an issue. Yet the question posed was regarding how much you let the most gifted player in Europe get away with off the field, before the side-effects became to much to tolerate.

Then on December 19th 1972, a meeting between all parties involved took place, which resulted in Frank O'Farrell being sacked as the manager of Manchester United, with George Best reportedly following him out of the door for good.

Tommy Docherty was appointed as the new manager and despite failing to win his first seven matches in charge at the club, a period of eight unbeaten games towards the end guided the club to safety with an 18th place finish, 5 points above the drop.

United started the 1973/74 season with a line-up which was barely recognisable to the team that conquered Europe just five years earlier, with the goalkeeper Alex Stepney being the only remnant from the Glory years of the late sixties. Charlton and Law had now moved on and United new-look team were once again struggling with only 3 wins in their first 12 matches of the new campaign. However during September the sensational news emerged that George Best would return to training, with both Tommy Docherty and the chairman Louis Edwards happy to have Best back in the side. His return to action came on October 20th 1973 in a 1-0 win over Birmingham City at Old Trafford, where Alex Stepney scored the winner after converting a penalty – the goalkeeper's second successful spot-kick of the season. Then against Tottenham Hotspur in a 2-1 defeat, the returning Irishman scored the first goal of his re-emergence in a flash of brilliance from old, when a weaving run past two defenders ended in a

20-yard drive whistling into the back of the net. He then netted in a 3-2 defeat to Coventry City at Old Trafford with another goal from outside the box, when he sold a dummy to two defenders before driving the ball into the bottom left of the goal.

However, these goals were amid a run of nine games without a win. The torrid sequence ended with a 2-0 win over Ipswich at Old Trafford on December 29th 1972 which proved to be George Best's last game in front of the home fans. United's next match ended in a 3-0 defeat to Queens Park Rangers on New Year's Day, which was the last time George Best was seen in a Manchester United shirt. The one-time European Player of the Year failed to report to training following the London fixture and despite turning up to United's next match against Plymouth Argyle in the F.A. Cup, a fall out with manager Tommy Docherty meant he was subsequently dropped from the team. After twelve and a half years at the club, George Best walked away for the final time, then sadly for Manchester United, the team were then relegated to Division Two at the end of the season.

Despite this cameo appearance in United's worst post-war season, George Best will be forever captured in time as the beatle-haired boy from Belfast who took the limits of what could be conjured with the heavy, sodden, leather orb of association football to a new level. His rise to greatness went from Earthly to mesospheric overnight after the Northern Irishman obliterated the unbeaten home record of the kings of Europe, Benfica, in 1966. He then became outer-worldly when he iconically walked the ball into the Benfica net in the European Cup final in 1968 with the number seven on his back. The same year he netted 32 goals and won the prestigious European Player of the Year Award. He became the third United player from the same team to achieve this and United's 'Holy Trinity' of Best, Law and Charlton became immortalised. He had the balance of a gymnast, the gait of a stallion and the way he glided past his opponents had an intangibility that had never been seen before. It was not just his actions on the field that made him so good, it was the way he made people feel. He would pack a usually half-filled stadium just because his name was in the starting eleven on the back of a match day programme. He embodied an air of freedom, embraced the reformism of the 1960's with his rebellious nature on the pitch and carried the dreams of the young people of this generation. George Best, quite simply the greatest footballer that ever lived.

BRYAN ROBSON

Pure Gold

In his early days with West Bromwich Albion, three leg breaks inside a year threatened Bryan Robson's future. Yet as a young man he demonstrated a determination that caught the eyes of many in English football, as he somehow made a complete recovery. He had appeared in nearly 200 league games for the Baggies, scoring 39 goals, when new United boss Ron Atkinson paid his former club a joint fee of around £2 million to bring both Robson and Remi Moses to Old Trafford in October 1981. With Robson's price tag an estimated £1.5 million, this became a British transfer fee record at the time.

Bryan Robson moved to United on 1 October 1981 and signed the record contract on the Old Trafford pitch two days later, The record was not broken for six years, when Liverpool paid £1.9 million for Newcastle striker Peter Beardsley in the summer of 1987. Many of those involved in football saw the transfer as a massive gamble, with the combination of the record price tag and Robson's track record of injuries with West Brom. Ron Atkinson's retort to that opinion was "It's not a gamble buying a player like Bryan Robson, because he's pure gold."

Robson made his first appearance for United against Tottenham Hotspur in the League Cup on October 7th 1981, where United lost 1-0 and his league debut for his new club came three days later, in a goalless draw against Manchester City at Maine Road. This was also his first appearance in the Manchester United number seven shirt. Robson's introduction to the team came amid a good run of form for the Reds, as they went twelve league games unbeaten, with Robson appearing in the last six. His first goal for United came on November 7th 1981 in a 5-1 win over Sunderland at Roker Park, which was all the more sweeter for the North Easterner who grew up supporting Newcastle United.

It was evident in his early matches that there was something strikingly extraordinary about Bryan Robson. His stamina saw him appear all over the pitch, putting his body on the line in one instant to help his team mates defend, before appearing in the opposition box moments later to score a goal. He never shirked a tackle, and seemingly enjoyed taking bullets for the team, crashing into every challenge like the world counted on him winning it. His early leadership qualities were there for all to see and United's new midfielder looked ready to lead his men out of the shadows of the Merseyside rule. A gladiator had arrived in Manchester and Old Trafford was his arena. In his first season for the Reds he only missed one match since he signed, whilst wearing the number seven jersey throughout the whole campaign since his league debut.

He became the first non-winger at Manchester United to make the revered shirt his own; and perhaps a change in the true meaning of the shirt evolved on the day as he first claimed ownership of it. Robson finished the season on a high after scoring in the final game of the season in a 2-0 win over Stoke City. The other scorer that day was a teenager called Norman Whiteside who became United's youngest ever goal scorer. Robson appeared to link up well with the Northern Irishman and perhaps it was an omen for things to come. In all, Robbo scored five goals in 32 appearances for the Reds as United finished third in the league.

Robson's worth was then seen on the international stage that summer when he went to the World Cup with the England national team. He scored after just 27 seconds in England's first game against France. It was the fastest goal ever scored in the World Cup finals and that record was to stand for some 20 years.

When the 1982/1983 campaign kicked off, Robson was starting his first full season for United. In a year full of promise, the United number seven wasted no time in making an impact by scoring in a 3-0 win over Nottingham Forest in the second league game of the season. He then netted another goal three days later against his former club West Bromwich Albion, although United ended up losing 3-1. Robson then scored his third goal in four games in a 2-1 win over Everton at

Old Trafford.

United made their first venture into Europe with Robson in the side when they faced a two-legged tie against Valencia in the UEFA Cup. After a stalemate at Old Trafford, United took the lead in the away leg after Robson powered home a brave flying header early in the match. The United number seven flew at the ball with the goalkeeper charging, however, his bravery paid off by putting the Reds1-0 up. Despite this, Ron Atkinson's team eventually lost 2-1 to the Spanish side.

United were still fighting on three fronts domestically and their league form continued to impress. After Robson scored the winner against Stoke City in a 1-0 win he then scored in a 3-0 victory over Norwich City at Old Trafford. This sparked a series of six matches without conceding a goal, and it was evident that the stability and steel that Robson brought to the United side was making them increasingly difficult to beat. During this run, a 4-0 win over Notts County at Old Trafford on December 11th 1982 saw Robson produce his finest performance to date. After creating the opening goal with a cutting cross-field ball which allowed Whiteside to score off an Arnold Muhren knock-down, he then had a hand in the third at both ends. After Robson won the ball back on the edge of his own box, he bamboozled two Notts County players, before releasing the ball for his team mates to attack. Rather than stand and watch, he then ran the full length of the field before appearing in the opponent's box to plant a header into the top corner of the net. It was an astonishing display of box-to-box exhibitionism that proved the United number seven was one of Europe's most complete footballers.

At the turn of the year United went on a run of twelve games unbeaten, which saw them reach the final of the League Cup, the quarter-final of the F.A. Cup and inch closer towards Liverpool at the top of the Division One table. Amid this sequence of results Robson scored in back-to back games, first against Birmingham City on January 15th 1983, then against Nottingham Forest four days later in a 4-0 win in the League Cup 5th Round. This meant that United would now face Arsenal in a two-legged semi-final.

The first leg of this tie at Highbury saw Bryan Robson produce another barn-storming performance for United in a 4-2 win. The

United number seven started the moves for three of United's goals, which gave them a huge advantage going into the return game at Old Trafford. The second leg was a bitter-sweet occasion for the Reds, as they progressed to the final with a 2-1 win, however Robson's tenacity in this match which was intended to drag his teammates to Wembley back-fired, as the United midfielder tore his ankle ligaments. Robson's combative style meant he ran the risk of injuring himself, yet it was this attitude of never holding back that made the United number seven a priceless commodity. As a result he missed the next nine matches in all competitions; and despite the Reds winning the Manchester Derby on March 5th 1983 and then the quarter-final of the F.A. Cup a week later, their league form started to suffer. Then on March 26th 1983 they lost the League Cup final 2-1 to Liverpool. United made a good start in this match with Norman Whiteside giving the Reds an early lead, however, the league leaders came back to win 2-1. It was evident that the steel and grit that may have taken United over the finishing line was perhaps missing due to the absence of Robson during this run of matches.

Robbo's return to action came in a Division One match against Southampton where he scored in a 1-1 draw at Old Trafford. The next match for Big Ron's team came against Arsenal in the F.A. Cup semi-final at Villa Park, where the Reds were looking to rectify their League Cup final loss by getting to Wembley once more. However, their plans seemed to be scuppered early on when Arsenal took the lead in the first half. Yet five minutes into the second half, Ashley Grimes swung in a cross from the left of midfield, where Robson chested the ball down, instantly beat his marker, then slotted a left foot drive past George Wood in the Arsenal goal. Robson could have scored another with his head, however, Wood pulled off a spectacular save. It was Whiteside who grabbed the second with a dipping volley and even though Kevin Moran was stretchered off with his head pouring with blood, Robson and his teammates held on to get to Wembley for the second time this season. United eventually finished in third place in Division One, with Robson netting another league goal in a 2-1 win over Swansea City at Old Trafford along the way. An F.A. Cup final now beckoned for Robson and the rest of the team as they travelled to Wembley to face Brighton and Hove Albion.

After a subdued performance, United drew 2-2 in the first match on May 21st 1983 with goals from Stapleton and Wilkins. The Reds were lucky that the game went to a replay, as Brighton should have won the cup in the last minute of extra-time when Gordon Smith had a clear shot on goal, however, Gary Bailey saved his attempt.
Five days later Robson performed heroically in the return leg and it was the United captain who opened the scoring after 25 minutes, when he struck the ball low to the keeper's left from outside the box. Whiteside made it 2-0 five minutes later, before Robson gave Ron Atkinson's men a 3-0 half-time lead when he poached his second goal from close-range, after following up his own header which Gordon McQueen knocked-back across goal.

If there was ever an example of a player sacrificing his own glory for the greater good of the team, then it occurred in the second half of this F.A. Cup final. Just after the hour mark, Manchester United were awarded a penalty after Robson won the ball back in his own half, then stormed forward into the Brighton penalty area off a Frank Stapleton pass. The United number seven was then hauled down by Brighton's Gary Stevens which resulted in a penalty. Bryan Robson now had the opportunity to become the first player to score a hat trick in an F.A. Cup final for thirty years, since Stan Mortenson netted three for Blackpool in 1953, yet Robson allowed United's regular penalty taker Arnold Muhren to take the spot-kick to ensure victory for the Reds. Muhren duly made it an emphatic 4-0 score-line and Robson walked up the Wembley steps to lift his first trophy for the Reds as captain.

United's number seven perfected the art of being a selfless footballer whilst inadvertently stealing the headlines for his performances. He was a leader who would rather see his own body damaged than let an opponent have the ball. He defended when it mattered, and he scored when it mattered. Moreover, in a world where footballers seemed to be regimented in their playing position with a sheep-like conformism, Bryan Robson became the team's sacrificial lamb whilst somehow ripping up the footballer's manual by appearing in every position on the field. The number seven jersey had now gone through a semantic change.

George Best made the shirt special because he happened to play in the position for which the number was allocated on several historic occasions, most importantly in the final 1968. Yet now it started to mean a lot more than merely playing on the wing, it now started to mean something else. Intriguingly, the number was slowly becoming just as important as the player who wore it.

The 1983/84 season started with a bang for Bryan Robson when Manchester United won the Charity Shield on August 20th 1983. The United captain netted both goals that day, the first coming from a through ball by Ray Wilkins which Robson latched on to before rounding Bruce Grobbelaar to score after 23 minutes. He then sealed the victory in the second half when he bundled the ball over the line after Gordon McQueen's header deflected into his direction. He then walked up the Wembley steps for the second competitive game in a row, to lift more silverware for the Reds as captain of the side.

Captain Marvel

Robson's first league goal of the season came on September 6th 1983 when he scored in a thrilling 3-2 win over Arsenal at Highbury. After a decent start in the league which saw them win four of their first five Division One matches, United's attention then turned to Europe where they faced Dukla Prague in the first round of the European Cup Winners' Cup on September 14th 1983. After a nervy 1-1 draw at Old Trafford United then travelled to Prague, where their European adventure seemed to be heading towards and early ending when the home side took the lead. Yet with Bryan Robson on the field anything seemed possible, so when the captain fired in a spectacular twenty-five yard equaliser soon after, United fans new that even the European stage would not faze their number seven. The Reds then took the lead through Stapleton before the hosts equalised, meaning United progressed to the next round via the away goals rule, after the score finished 2-2 on the night and 3-3 on aggregate. In the next round of the competition United were drawn against Spartak Varna where they played the away leg of this second round tie on October 19th 1983. Robson again scored a vital away goal in a 2-1 win over the Bulgarian side, before the Reds eventually progressed 4-1 on aggregate after a 2-0 win at Old Trafford. In between these two matches the United captain started a run which saw him score in four consecutive league matches, taking his total to nine for the season by the end of November. An injury meant he missed playing in most of the Christmas fixture list and his first game back in January was not a pleasant return for United's captain, as they failed to defend the F.A. Cup at the first hurdle by losing 2-0 to Harry Redknapp's Bournmouth in the third round. Despite this, United's league form was imperious and they went on a sixteen match unbeaten run in Division One, with Robson scoring five goals in ten games after the shock cup exit.

With Robson now firmly established as one of the best midfielders in Europe, he started to attract attention from the continent's big clubs. Rumours suggested that the United number seven was set to move to Italy, with A.C. Milan, Sampdoria and Juventus leading the race, however, this did not appear to affect his United form. Then on March 7th 1984, the Reds had to face a European giant of their own, in the form of a Barcelona side which boasted perhaps the world's best player, Diego Maradona. The first leg of the European Cup Winner's Cup quarter-final was at the Nou Camp in front of 94,000 spectators; and the Reds counted themselves to be a little unlucky as Graeme Hogg scored an own goal to put the home side in front. At one nil, the tie still seemed salvageable with the second leg at Old Trafford still to come, however, United suffered a body-blow when Juan Carlos Rojo scored Barcelona's second goal and gave the Spanish side a seemingly unassailable 2-0 lead.

The return game was held on March 21st 1984 in front of a packed Old Trafford. Before the match, thousands of United fans implored the club not let their hero Bryan Robson leave by the means of a petition. Many of those involved in football thought that Diego Maradona was going to have a field day at Old Trafford. Yet the belief of United fans was that their own Bryan Robson would be the man who could instigate any form of a comeback. As the game kicked-off in a cauldron of noise, United fans did not let the Barcelona players settle on the ball by booing and jeering their every touch, particularly reserving treatment for Maradona, who seemed knocked of his guard by the heckling.

Ron Atkinson's team lapped up the intensity of the atmosphere and after hitting the crossbar early on through Norman Whiteside, the home team continued to press which resulted in the opening goal of the game. In the 22nd minute, a swinging corner by Ray Wilkins was met by Graeme Hogg, who flicked the ball on for Robson to head home from close-range.

Now the Atmosphere cranked up a notch. The usual ripple and chorus of a normal football match was no longer heard. There became a shrill, dense wall of noise that had never been heard before at Old Trafford. It was an enchanting din that echoed around all four sides of the stadium, like a thick, haunted forest packed with forty thousand piercing eyes and shrieking voices that surrounded a clearing of green. The surrealism of the support was absorbed by the United players, who did not give Barcelona any time to settle on the ball. Five minutes into the second half their persistence paid off, as a nervy back-pass by Victor Munoz enabled Whiteside to force Barcelona's goalkeeper Urruti into a mistake, which saw the ball break to Remi Moses, whose cross allowed Wilkins to shoot on goal. The ball was only parried out by the goalkeeper before Robson instinctively and heroically slid in to score the equaliser.

A growing crescendo of bellowing noise became bedlam less than a minute later when United made it 3-0 after Arthur Albiston's cross was met by Whiteside, who nodded the ball into the path of Stapleton for the Irishman to power home the third.

The rapturous support became a wailing of idolatry for their captain Bryan Robson as United held on to progress to the semi-finals of the competition. The United number seven was carried off the pitch on a human throne of Manchester United supporters whom did not want their hero to ever abdicate. It was United's greatest European night to date since they won the European Cup in 1968 and the fans had a new idol. He was the first player since George Best that had the hero status of a saviour; and he wore the same number in this match that Best wore against Benfica.

The number seven shirt was now a garment that could only be reserved for a player who could take the club into the heights of fantasy. It was not just a football jersey anymore; it was a symbol of greatness. It was the touchable power source that represented the romance and philosophy of the club. It seemed as though the nucleus of which the magic of Manchester United spawned from was circulating around the threads of the shirt.

Four days before the first leg of the semi-final, which was to be played at Old Trafford against Juventus, United beat Birmingham City 1-0 with Robson scoring the only goal of the game. After this match it was reported that the United captain had suffered a hamstring injury and as a result he would miss both legs of the Juventus tie.

More ominously for the Reds, whilst Robson was in Turin for the second leg he was given the go-ahead by the club to speak to Juventus about a potential move away from Old Trafford. Thankfully for United fans, the proposed transfer never materialised as Juventus and the rest of the potential buyers were put-off by United's £3 million valuation price. Robbo's injury also caused him to miss some games in the domestic ruin-in which saw United slip to a fourth place finish. Yet the good news was that Bryan Robson was staying at Manchester United and he was staying for good, as he signed a seven year contract worth around £1 million which meant he would stay with the club until at least 1991.

The 1984/85 season started well for Ron Atkinson's men as they went unbeaten in their first eleven matches in all competitions. During this run, Robson netted his first league goal of the season in a 3-0 win away to Coventry, before scoring the first goal in the first leg of the UEFA Cup first round against Raba Vasas in another 3-0 scoreline.

The captain then led United to the next round of the UEFA Cup when the Reds drew 2-2 in the second leg against the Hungarian side. In between these matches, Robson scored in a 4-0 win over Burnley in the League Cup second round and a vital goal in a 2-1 win over his former club West Bromwich Albion in the league.

The season was again simmering nicely as the Reds were still fighting on three fronts despite an early exit in the League Cup at the hands of Everton. Manchester United's success still seemed dependent on whether their number seven remained free from injury and whether he would perform. The evidence suggested that if Robson played and performed in every match, then the possibilities for United were endless. However, his rambunctious style meant that he always ran the risk of harming himself. It was a paradox that was perhaps frustrating for many fans, as if Robson was to play at his peak, then the odds were eventually stacked in favour of him sustaining an injury. If he played in a reserved manner with the intent of self-preservation, then he would no longer be the same player. If you took the fire out of his belly, then he would not be able to slay the dragons in front of him.

United progressed to the third round of the UEFA Cup after a 1-0 aggregate win over PSV Eidhoven, which meant they would face a two-legged tie against Dundee United. On November 28th 1984 Robson scored in the first leg at Old Trafford against the Scottish side, which resulted in a 2-2 draw, before captaining his side to a 3-2 win at Tannadice which meant qualification to the quarter-finals. In between these European ties, the United captain then scored four goals in his next seven Division One matches, however, at the turn of the year Robson was again side-lined through injury meaning he missed the next ten matches for the Reds. Robson did not return to action again that season until March 9th 1985, yet United played well in his absence and progressed to the semi-finals of the F.A.Cup, whilst winning the first leg of their UEFA Cup quarter-final match against Videoton 1-0. Robson scored on his return from injury in a 2-2 draw with West Ham, yet United's next match saw them eliminated from the UEFA Cup on penalties, after losing 1-0 to Videoton in Hungary during the second leg. Manchester United now had their sights set on another trip to Wembley and Robson remaining fit seemed key to this ambition, as they faced the reigning champions Liverpool in the last four of the F.A. Cup.

On April 13th 1985 the Reds travelled to Goodison Park to face their north-west rivals in the much awaited semi-final. Once again it Bryan Robson's penchant for the big occasion that helped him to break the deadlock mid-way through the second half, when he latched on to a Gordon Strachan corner at the far post. As the midfield maestro steered the ball goalwards, it appeared to take a deflection of Mark Hughes, however, it was the captain who claimed the goal and it was his timely arrival in the box that helped to open the scoring. A Liverpool equaliser forced the game into extra time and then another late equaliser in this period, which cancelled out a Stapleton goal, meant the game went to a replay.

The return match at Main Road had the same fervent atmosphere in the terraces, which insulated the heated action on the pitch. United were 1-0 down going into the second half before a moment of individual genius levelled the game for the Reds. After receiving the ball in the centre circle, Robson exchanged a one-two with Frank Stapleton before he ran towards the Liverpool goal. With nobody up in support, the United captain unleashed a 25 yard shot which whirled into the top corner of the net. Bryan Robson had pulled another rabbit out of the hat on the big stage, with his conjury putting Ron Atkinson's men on level terms in an F.A. Cup semi-final replay against the reigning champions of England. It was this flash of brilliance that heightened Robson to the level of a messiah; and perhaps the number seven shirt was now seen as the attire which was only to be worn by a chosen few. Mark Hughes then scored the winner for United meaning they would now face Everton in the F.A. Cup final. Just like the Barcelona game in the previous season, the full time whistle saw United fans flood onto the pitch to celebrate with their heroes. Robson was again the main focus of attention, with him being placed on a human pedestal as hundreds of fans carried him off the pitch. The number seven which adorned his white kit was seen rising above his idolaters like a flag at full mast, as the United midfielder was once more the commander in another gargantuan victory for the Reds.

United finished fourth in the league, just a point off second place after failing to win the last game of the season. Robson did not feature in the final three league matches of the season in preparation for the F.A. Cup final on May 18th 1985, against an Everton side that had won the league by a record points total and notched a victory in the European Cup Winner's Cup final three days before. Everton appeared to be on course for a treble of trophies when Kevin Moran was sent-off for United in the second half of normal time, however, Robson and his team stood firm. Then in the second period of extra time, Norman Whiteside curled in an unlikely winner which saw Bryan Robson lift the F.A. Cup for the second time as captain of Manchester United.

Spear-headed by Bryan Robson, Manchester United were not only challenging for the league, they were winning trophies as well. Despite this, winning the Division One title still remained an elusive achievement for Ron Atkinson's team. As for the main contenders Liverpool and Everton, who had been dominating domestically and who were both victorious in Europe in the 1984/1985 season, United had no trouble in beating them. The Red's had proved they were a match for England's and Europe's best during the first half of the eighties, yet it was beating the so-called lesser teams on the domestic scene that proved a stumbling block.

United now entered the 1985/1986 season knowing that consistency would be the key to mounting a serious title challenge; and as history had told them, keeping a fit Bryan Robson in the side would be a prerequisite for this to happen. After a disappointing 2-0 defeat to Everton in the Charity Shield, United then went on a Division One Rampage. The Reds won their first ten league matches in a row, with an ever-present and influential Bryan Robson captaining the side. United were blowing the opposition away with 27 goals being scored in this opening run of games. It was not until November 2nd 1985 that the Reds lost their first fixture, after an eighteen match unbeaten run in league and cup football, with a 1-0 defeat to Sheffield Wednesday at Hillsborough. This had Manchester United fans believing that they could finally end their nineteen year wait for the Division One title. Moreover, with the Reds not participating in the European Cup Winner's Cup due to a ban on English clubs playing in European competition after the Heysel disaster, Big Ron's team could firmly concentrate on their domestic calendar.

Many believed that United's number seven Bryan Robson would be the man to guide the team back to the pinnacle of English football. Yet this notion seemed a disservice to the rest of the Manchester United players, insinuating that they could not win anything without their captain. The United fans were blessed with personnel who were a class apart from most of the Division's footballers, with the likes of Norman Whiteside, Paul McGrath, Gordon Strachan and Mark Hughes lighting up Old Trafford. However, whereas these players could hit footballing heights that no other player could reach, it became evident that any player who could comfortably carry the revered number seven on their back was the one who could hit heights that had not yet been imagined. Manchester United's last league triumph in 1966/1967 was achieved by a team which contained Bobby Charlton, Denis Law, Nobby Stiles, Bill Foulkes and Paddy Crerend.

Yet George Best's prodigal wizardry had never been seen before and this unknown quantity was regarded as the extra element that helped steer Matt Busby's team to domestic and European glory. United knew that without Robson they still had a winning formula; however, with their captain this formula became more potent, which gave them an extra edge as they contested against the perpetual winners on Merseyside.

Unfortunately, Robson missed most of the Christmas period through injury. This coincided with a slump in form, causing United to be eliminated by Liverpool in the League Cup fifth round, whilst losing four more league games in his absence. Robson then made a brief return to action, where the Reds progressed to the last sixteen of the F.A. Cup at the expense of Sunderland after a replay. The United captain then scored a league goal in a 2-1 defeat to West Ham, which saw the Reds slip from the number one spot for the first time since the start of the season. Then on March 5th 1986 Robson suffered a dislocated shoulder in a 1-1 draw away to West Ham in the F.A. Cup fifth round, just three minutes into the game. As the skipper disappeared down the tunnel in agony, it was felt that Manchester United's title chances disappeared with him. The Reds were eliminated from the F.A. Cup in Robson's absence with a 2-0 defeat in the replay at Old Trafford, before losing further ground in the league. The United number seven made a few fleeting appearances during March and April, however, the damage had already been done. The Reds finished in fourth place for the third season running and the United manager and several of the players were soon brought into question.

A Match Made In Heaven

In the summer before the 1986/1987 season Robson suffered a personal low, when a re-occurrence of his shoulder injury whilst playing for England in the group stages of the 1986 World Cup in Mexico forced him to miss the rest of the tournament. This also meant that the United captain missed the first four games of the new campaign, where the Reds only managed to amass one point from four games. Upon his return, United won their first match of the season with a 5-1 win over Southampton at Old Trafford. Despite this,

United's poor form continued as they failed to win any of their next four league matches, albeit Robson did score a superb long range volley in a 3-1 loss to Everton at Goodison Park on September 21st 1986, before netting another in a 1-1 draw away to Nottingham Forest two weeks later. The Red's appeared to turn a corner as they stayed unbeaten in the month of October, which saw them progress to the third round of the League Cup at the expense of Port Vale with a 7-2 aggregate victory and enabled them to climb the Division One table.

Robson then suffered another spell on the sidelines through injury; and his absence was consequential once again as on November 4th 1986 United crashed out of the League Cup with a 4-1 loss to Southampton in a third round replay. Two days later, Ron Atkinson was sacked as Manchester United manager after a dismal run of form. As a result, a decision had to be made as to who would replace Big Ron at the Old Trafford helm. This prompted the board to appoint the Aberdeen manager Alex Ferguson, a man who had broken up the Old Firm duopoly at the top of the Scottish league and delivered European success with the club. Whether a manager from north of the border could re-enact the same success in English football remained to be seen, but what the new boss brought was a ruthless desire to win football matches; a character trait which Bryan Robson exuded on the football pitch. Perhaps now the United captain had found the perfect footballing matrimony with his new manager.

The origins of many of the club's successful era's have derived from appointments of managers and players alike, followed by an aspect of pioneering. Matt Busby's appointment enabled him to be the first manager to play untried youngsters who won trophies whilst entertaining the crowd. This vision became the philosophy of the club, yet it somehow became lost in the glamour of modern times, when extravagance and big money signings became the theme of the eighties. Despite the two F.A. Cup victories that Ron Atkinson achieved, it was hard to envisage United winning the league title any time soon and there never seemed to be any suggestion of long-term dominance. Bryan Robson was a leader amongst men on the field and he could spur his teammates on to win any given fixture on any given day, yet the consistency required by all eleven players was lacking over the duration of a full season. What they needed was a leader of men off the field, and if Alex Ferguson could live up to his ambition, then English football would be on the cusp of a cataclysmic change.

The immediate task in hand for United was to climb away from the relegation places, yet as Robson missed the first four matches of Ferguson's tenure, United continued with a poor run of form. Upon the captain's return the Red's started to up their game and after two back-to-back 3-3 thrillers against Tottenham Hotspur and Aston Villa at the start of December, United then ended the year on a high with a 1-0 victory over Liverpool on Boxing Day. Robson's first goal under the new manager came in the Manchester Derby on March 7th 1987 at Old Trafford, with the United number seven relishing the big occasion once more. Another ghost like arrival in the box saw Robson convert a Peter Davenport cross to help secure a 2-0 victory over their city rivals. This was was the catalyst for the United captain to go on another goalscoring run as he netted a week later in a 2-1 defeat against Luton Town, before scoring in consecutive home games. His first came in a 2-0 win over Nottingham Forest and then a decisive goal in a 3-2 win over Oxford United saw the Reds all but ensure First Division safety. Robson added another to his season's tally of seven goals with a superbly taken strike against Aston Villa at Old Trafford on the final day of the 1986/1987 season. All those associated with United could now only look forward to the next campaign.

The new manager was now becoming renowned for ruling with an no-nonsense style, yet he shared the same steely-eyed ambition that smouldered inside his captain Bryan Robson. The United number seven was enthusiastically described as pure gold by his previous manager, and with the new iron-fisted boss working with him in tandem, it had the potential to produce an alloy of success, which could see this United team challenge for the league title once more.

The 1987/1988 season was a pivotal one for Bryan Robson as the United captain was now thirty years old and despite his achievements in football, the United captain still had a lot of unfinished business on the football field. An injury laden career had left Robson with a lot of what ifs hanging over his record, however, with a new manager at Old Trafford starting his first full season, there was now a platform for the United number seven to fulfil many of his burning ambitions as a footballer.

United remained unbeaten in their first seven league games, with Robson's first goalscoring contribution coming in a 3-1 victory away to Charlton Athletic on August 29th 1987. After new signing Bryan McClair opened the scoring for the Reds at the Valley, Robson added a second after winning the ball back in his own half, when Charlton were on an attack of their own. After United broke forward, McClair saw his shot saved, only for Robson to pounce and score amid a clatter of Charlton defenders. Robson's goal proved he had the same unrelenting desire to win as he ever had; and the fact that his timely interception was conducive to him scoring at the other end of the field proved that he was still worth two players on the pitch.

United lost their first game of the season at Everton on September 19th 1987, however, the Reds did not lie down and after they progressed past Hull City in the first round of the League Cup, they continued with their impressive league form. On October 10th 1987 Robson netted the opening goal in an impressive 4-2 away win over Sheffield Wednesday after a loose ball broke to him in the penalty area. He then unselfishly set- up McClair to score United's fourth. Then a week later the United captain scored the decisive second goal against Norwich City in a 2-1 victory, where he became bravery personified once again. Late in the game, Bryan McClair swung in a cross, which was met by Robson, whose gravity-defying leap saw him power a header past Bryan Gunn, before the United number seven fell into a crumpled heap on the ground. Instead of celebrating, the man known as Captain Marvel just writhed in agony, yet this was the price Bryan Robson often paid for victory and for him, the cost seemed well worth the resulting prize. It was now evident that no player in the history of the game had played with such sacrifice. One can only surmise that Robson was so mentally tuned in to winning, that he forgot about himself physically. His header was like a kamikaze pilot, intent on sacrificing himself for the greater good of victory.

Robson then netted an exquisite long-range, left-footer two weeks later against Nottingham Forest at Old Trafford in the league, before adding two more goals to his tally in December. The captain's fine form coincided with United putting a run together which saw them only lose two games in the league and cup before Christmas. This type of consistency coupled with an injury-free Robson meant that title winning talk was back on the agenda for those inside Old Trafford. A win-at-all-costs captain was now being governed by a win-at-all-costs manager; and only time would tell as to when the rewards would be reaped.

United's indifferent start to the new year meant that second place in the league would be the highest they could realistically finish this season. The Reds were then eliminated from the League Cup by Oxford in January and lost to Arsenal in the F.A. Cup fifth round a month later, meaning that there would be no silverware for Fergie's team this year. Bryan Robson was absent from this clash with the Gunners, which meant once again United failed to win a big match without their influential skipper. So many times throughout the eighties Manchester United crumbled on the big stage without Bryan Robson in the team, which equated to a decade of fans pondering what might have been. Yet they still had unfinished business in the league and United kicked into gear going into the final stretch of the season.

Having won three out of four games in March, which included a goal from Robson in a 3-1 win over West Ham, United then travelled to Anfield on 4th April 1988 to face the league's leaders Liverpool. Many times throughout the eighties United found it bizarrely easy to beat Liverpool, even though the Merseysiders where quite often considered to be the best team in Europe during this epoch. With Liverpool having a healthy lead at the top of the table, it was once again the prize of bragging rights that were up for grabs for United. True to form it was the Reds who took the lead and once again it was United's number seven who rose to the occasion. After a Davenport cross, the United captain met the ball in the six yard box after a darting run, before exquisitely lifting the ball over Bruce Grobbelaar with his left foot to open scoring. This seemed to be a false dawn as Liverpool struck back with three goals and looked like they would cruise to victory with a scoreline which would reflect their brutish dominance of English football. The Reds appeared to lose their discipline as Norman Whiteside clattered Liverpool's Steve McMahon, before Colin Gibson was sent off for a second bookable offence. Yet Robson, who was tailor-made for the blood bath that ensued, found a moment of inspiration when his twenty five yard shot deflected its way into the Liverpool goal. The United number seven had given his team the unlikeliest of lifelines and his two goals proved that no team, whoever they may be, would cause Robson to shrink back and accept the situation. This was a player who could single handedly inspire his teammates to match any team in the world, no matter how dire the circumstances may seem. His goals set-up the platform for Gordon Strachan to equalise, with the Scotsman cheekily celebrating with an imaginary cigar in front of the Kop. The draw prompted United to remain unbeaten for the rest of the season and it exhibited that Bryan Robson still had the same drive and passion that he had previously exuded throughout his United career.

There are times when the world of football tilts slightly on its axis allowing the sun to shine on the next fairytale while the old story ebbs slowly away into the shade. This Robson inspired performance could not be seen as just another occasion where United had upped their game to get one over their bitter rivals. Many now saw this as a sign of events to come. For Alex Ferguson and his captain, this staggering comeback with ten men against the best team around would be a shuddersome prophesy. Robson then added two more goals to his tally in the final weeks as United finished runners-up to Liverpool, before the number seven jetted off to the European Championships with England.

With Manchester United finishing second, it appeared that only a few minor tweaks to the team would see Fergie guide the Reds Devils to the title once more. However, the United boss started to make drastic changes to the squad and introduced more youngsters into the set-up as the 1988/1989 season got underway. This meant that Bryan Robson and many of the other senior players saw their place in the side under threat for the first time. Furthermore the captain was now entering a season which would see him turn 32 in January, with his age and injury record causing doubt as to whether his high octane performances could last for much longer.

United failed to win their first two games of the season, yet on September 10th 1988, Robson netted the winner in their first victory of the season with a deft twenty-yarder at home to Middlesbrough, before scoring in a 2-0 win away to Luton Town a week later. His next two goals came in the League Cup, with one in the second round against Rotherham in a 5-0 win at Old Trafford, followed by another in a 2-1 defeat to Wimbledon in early November. This League Cup exit only compounded the misery of going nine games without a league win throughout October and November. United, who finished second the season before, now found themselves flirting with relegation with the same squad as the previous season, barring the record re-signing of Mark Hughes, who's £1.8 million pound transfer eclipsed Bryan Robson's fee back in 1981. As a consequence it was widely felt that several of United's star players from the eighties were no longer cutting it at the highest level. Injuries and age seemed to take its toll on Fergie's big names, however, the manager himself sought an ulterior reason for this decline; and soon many of the fan's favourites and players who seemed untouchable, including Bryan Robson, now suspected that their careers at Manchester United were now coming to an end.

A certain drinking culture that was rife amongst English football in this era was allegedly embraced by many of the star players at Old Trafford. It was said that the main participants in this pass-time were fan favourites Norman Whiteside, Paul McGrath and more controversially the captain Bryan Robson. When these stars were available for selection they invariably played, however, the strict manager's iron fist was about to be slammed down on the Old Trafford playing staff, causing a shock-wave that would produce an inescapable reverberation for anyone inside Manchester United.

The Reds form improved in the new year as four wins on the bounce in the league saw them climb the table. United also started to put together a cup run, with Robson scoring in both the third and fourth round of the F.A Cup. United were eliminated in the quarter-finals against Nottingham Forest at Old Trafford then went on a run of only one win in nine games. This dreadful run of games ensured United finished eleventh in the Division One table, in a forgettable season which prompted the manager to ruthlessly swing the axe.

Norman Whiteside, Paul McGrath and Gordon Strachan were all given their marching orders; and Remi Moses retired through injury. This decision was an unpopular one for the fans, however, the manager felt a shake-up was needed. The members of the drinking club that Fergie believed to have existed had been off-loaded barring one alleged member of that society – Bryan Robson. It was evident that rather than being problematic, he remained enigmatic. Despite the United captain's endeavours in his social life, his performances and die-for-the-cause mentality never wavered. His penchant for a pint may not have mirrored George Best's glitzy champagne lifestyle, however, his jaunts to the pub with mates made his displays for Manchester United even more startling. He was quite often a one-man band on the football pitch, yet the United number seven was not required to face the music that awaited several of his colleagues. Robson was a one-off, he had an unerring abundance of professionalism when the number seven of Manchester United was emblazoned his back; and now he would become United's lasting relic from the days of yore, an artefact from old times, who's footballing sorcery would lead the new youngsters of Manchester United into a brave new world; and who would become a symbol of idolatry for the fans inside Old Trafford.

The 1989/1990 season started with Bryan Robson facing serious competition for his place in the side for the first time in his career, as midfielders Neil Webb, Paul Ince and Mike Phelan joined Manchester United in big money transfer deals. Despite this, Robson still remained first choice in the centre of the pitch for the Reds and on the opening day of the season United beat reigning champions Arsenal 4-1 at Old Trafford, with Robson starting the game as captain and wearing the number seven shirt which was still exclusively his.

With a crushing victory over last season's Divison One winners and the influx of new high profile players, there became the expectation that United could mount a challenge good enough to win the league for the first time in 23 years. Robson's impact remained as potent as ever as the United captain scored in a 1-1 draw with Crystal Palace three days later. However, the hype surrounding the start of the season soon appeared to be a false dawn as United lost their next three league fixtures. United's domestic reprieve came in a 5-1 mauling of Millwall at Old Trafford on September 16th 1989 with Robson scoring the second goal after another classic strike to add to his bulging scrapbook, as he curled the ball into the top corner from the edge of the box. The hope and expectation which surrounded the early days of the new season had been temporarily reignited and now the Reds travelled to Maine Road for the Manchester Derby, in what would be the ultimate test of temperament for several of Robson's new teammates, as the United number seven had been ruled out of the clash through injury. What prevailed was United's most humiliating defeat under their new boss Ferguson and also their biggest Derby defeat since 1955. Many of United's stars had buckled under the pressure; and without their Trojan-esque leader, they once again failed to conquer the task of winning a big football match. Despite the different players and the change in manager, it seemed that that Robson was still Manchester United's most influential player and he was still the man for the main occasions. However, the flames that burned so brightly at the start of the campaign had now been extinguished in the worst possible fashion, with the optimism turning to trepidation, even at this early stage of the season.

Upon Robson's return to the side United managed to amass thirteen points from their next six matches which consolidated their league position in the top half of the table, yet after beating Luton Town on November 18th 1989, Fergie's men failed to win any of their next eleven league matches in a run which stretched until early February. To make matters worse the United captain was once again sidelined through injury at the end of December, causing him to watch painfully as his beloved team were sucked into the relegation zone.

With the new multi-million pound signings failing to produce on the pitch and Robson watching helplessly from the sidelines, it became clear that the manager's position at the club was being called into question by many fans. An early exit from the League Cup at the hands of Tottenham Hotspur halted any realistic chances of silverware and it was evident that the team were a million miles away from challenging for the league. With injuries plaguing another season for the United number seven and a crop of new flopping players in the team, it seemed that a fairytale ending to his career was a far-fetched pipe-dream that even the biggest footballing romanticists could not envisage. Yet amid this alleged crisis, there remained one iota of hope that perhaps was brushed away amid the misery of a turgid season.

On January 7th Manchester United faced Nottingham Forest in the third Round of the F.A. Cup without a win in eight games and without their captain Bryan Robson. Even the television commentators that day claimed that United looked like a 'beaten team' in the warm-up before the game had even started. However, somehow the players managed to galvanise themselves to produce a shock 1-0 win over the reigning League Cup winners and all-round cup specialists Forest on their own patch. Mark Robins scored the winner and for the time being, the boss and the big money players had momentary respite from their ardent detractors. It was also suggested that this win prevented manager Ferguson from being sacked, a notion which was later denied by the board at Old Trafford.

Amid this treacherous run of results in Division One, United beat F.A. Cup giant-killers Hereford 1-0 at Edgar Street in the next round of the cup, before winning 3-2 away to Newcastle United in round 5. Fergie's men then progressed to the semi-finals at the expense of Sheffield United at Bramall Lane with a 1-0 win. Remarkably, all these matches were away from home. Yet United's league form still meant that their first Division status was far from safe going into March. What it did display, however, was that there was something more than ordinary about this team. When their back's were against the wall and they needed to fight for their manager and their reputation, they somehow pulled off a cup run of doggedness and inspiration that was only previously seen throughout the last decade, when the team were being driven by the gallantry of their captain Bryan Robson.

On April 8th 1990 Manchester United set-out to play Oldham Athletic in the semi-final of the F.A. Cup at Maine Road - a ground where they had been trounced 5-1 by its tenants Manchester City earlier in the season. Bryan Robson was making his first start this side of Christmas and he lit-up the grand spectacle once more, by equalising for the Reds after Oldham took an early lead. Once the captain was set clear on goal, there was never any doubt that he would show the composure to get United back into to the game. This also meant that Robson astonishingly scored in his third consecutive F.A. Cup Semi- Final. The Reds ended up drawing 3-3 in a topsy turvy game which meant that a replay would be held three days later at the same ground. This time Robson and his team won 2-1 after extra time with Mark Robins scoring the winner.

It had been an incredible turn of fortunes for United and Bryan

Robson. After staring relegation in the face in March, the United number seven returned to a side which won four league games on the bounce and progressed to the F.A. Cup final. Robson now had the chance to captain Manchester United in the final for the third time, which could consolidate his legendary status as a Manchester United player. This also proved that the Manchester United number seven shirt could now only been donned by a player who had at least the slightest hint of Bryan Robson's or George Bests's majesty.

On May 12th 1990 Manchester United would now face Crystal Palace in the F.A. Cup final. It was United's first chance of silverware since they last won the competition in 1985; and the only surviving players from that day were Mark Hughes and Bryan Robson. United gave themselves an uphill struggle after conceding an early goal, yet the imperious captain made his mark on yet another monumental occasion. With 10 minutes of the first half to play, Robson equalised for Manchester United with a back post header from a Bryan McClair cross. This gave his team, who were playing in all white this day, the much needed impetus to add some colour to the long awaited Wembley occasion. The rest of the game became a nervy affair with United taking the lead after a Mark Hughes goal, before Palace substitute Ian Wright made it 2-2. Wright then then gave the opposition the lead in extra-time until Hughes forced a replay with a timely equaliser.

The second match saw United play in their more familiar red kit and Robson put in what was now an expected performance of inspired leadership and midfield mastery. However, the winning goal came from an unexpected source; the United left-back Lee Martin. It was his strike an hour into the game which saw the Reds win 1-0 at Wembley, which meant Robson would now go down in history as the first captain to lift the F.A. Cup on three separate occasions; and each time he would be wearing the number seven shirt. He became a three-time conqueror, the undisputed king of knock-out football, the undisputed commander of the oldest competition in the world. His triple trophy lift which spanned seven years of his captaincy was conformation that he was the greatest leader of his generation. Surely now age and injuries were closing in on him, and the quest for more glory had to be burdened upon another man. Yet importantly, as the players around him started to come of age, maybe now his inspiration had finally filtered around the rest of the team.

What is more, Robson now had the chance to lead Manchester United into Europe once again, as English football's ban on participating in European competition would be lifted the following season.

The 1990/1991 season was another injury hit campaign for Bryan Robson, as achilles and toe injuries which happened with England in the group stages of the 1990 World Cup in Italy meant Captain Marvel would not make an appearance until the end of December. His return was a timely one nonetheless, as United entered the new year still fighting on all four fronts. The Reds had already qualified for the quarter-finals of the European Cup Winner's Cup after seeing off Pecsi Munkas and Wrexham in the earlier rounds. Then despite an F.A Cup quarter-final defeat to Norwich City in February which meant United had failed to defend their trophy from the previous year, they still found a route to Wembley again with an aggregate victory over Leeds United in the League Cup semi-final.

Now European ambitions started to burn for Sir Alex Ferguson's men, after they overcame Montepelllier 3-1 on aggregate in their European Cup Winner's Cup quarter-final tie, which meant they would now face Polish cup winners Legia Wasaw in the last four of the competition. In between these two legs, the United captain scored his only goal of the season in a 3-1 win against Derby County at Old Trafford on April 16th 1991. Yet five days later Robson suffered a career low after being beaten 1-0 by Sheffield Wednesday in the League Cup final which meant the legendary number seven suffered his first cup final defeat at Wembley. Perhaps the skipper, who was now 34, had seen his best days in the number seven shirt pass him by; and after United reached the European Cup Winners Cup final after beating Legia Warsaw 4-2 on aggregate, the question remained as to whether Bryan Robson had anything left in the tank.

On 15th May 1991 Manchester United lined-up against Catalan giants Barcelona in the final of the European Cup Winner's Cup at the Feyenoord Stadium in Rotterdam. This was the first time that United had appeared in a European final since 1968 and the first time that captain Bryan Robson had faced the Spanish giants since his heroics in 1984, when the United fans carried him of the pitch in jubilation. The Reds went into this game as underdogs and with the attacking threat of Barcelona's Michael Laudrup and Julio Salenas to contend with, it was clear that United were in for a difficult night. However an out-of-the-box tactic deployed by the United manager was for Robson to man-mark Ronald Koeman, who was playing in a defensive role. Koeman was one of the classiest footballers of his generation and he was seen as the man who started most of Barcelona's attacks. The Dutchman also had the incentive of playing in his home country, which meant stopping him was going to be a tall order for anyone.

Nonetheless, When the orders are tall, it had been consistently one man who had stood the tallest in the preceding ten years at the club. The United number seven defied his years by stifling Koeman's creativity, whilst setting United on attacks of their own. Then on 67 minutes, United had a free-kick 40 yards from goal. Although Clayton Blackmore was eyeing-up a shot, the United captain took charge of proceedings and curled in a cross which landed on the head of Steve Bruce. The ball was heading into the goal before Mark Hughes made sure by prodding the ball home on the line to give the Reds a one-nil lead. Robson was at his rock solid finest, blunting any cutting edge that the opposition had in attack, whilst going forward he was razor sharp, which was splitting the silk of Barcelona's defence in two. The United number seven was now back at the vertex of his capabilities. He had jumped into the footballing portal and transported himself to the magical realm that is only befitting of a Manchester United number seven. On 74 minutes he picked the ball up on half way, before flaying a wondrous pass with the outside of his left boot, arcing it with pin-point accuracy into the path of Mark Hughes, who rounded the keeper and fired the ball into the net spectacularly from the acutest of angles.

It became a nervy ending for United after Koeman pulled a goal back with a late free-kick. Then a clearance off the line from Blackmore and a disallowed Barcelona goal kept the score at 2-1. Relief and euphoria ensued after the final whistle where Bryan Robson lifted his fourth piece of silverware as Manchester United captain. His three conquests of Wembley had now been outshone by leading his team to victory on a new battleground abroad. The travelling fans were singing in the rain as the heavens opened on the roofless stadium, soaking the sea of jubilant red support. Moreover, this also wetted the appetite of Robson and his teammates to win bigger and better things in the coming seasons; and it was safe to say that their trophy dry-spell had been well an truly broken.

On the opening day of the the 1991/1992 season Bryan Robson scored one of his best ever strikes, when he volleyed the ball into the top corner of the net from the edge of the box, in a 2-0 win over Notts County at Old Trafford. This seemed a good omen for United as Bryan Robson's influence in the heart of the midfield was still going to be as integral as ever. Two weeks later on August 31st 1991 he then netted a late equalizer against Leeds United in a 1-1 draw at Old Trafford, which meant United kept their unbeaten start to the season intact. By the end of September, the Reds stretched their unbeaten start to ten games, which was marked by a Bryan Robson winner against Tottenham Hotspur at White Hart Lane. On this day in London, the United number seven converted a long-range header from a Clayton Blackmore free-kick, which gave United all three points and a spot at the top of the league.

After going another two games unbeaten in the league, and conceding only four league goals since the start of the season, United notched up their first defeat of the campaign away to Sheffield Wednesday at the end of October in a 3-2 defeat. Title winning talk was now firmly being thrown about, yet trepidation still existed as the Reds had been in this position before and failed to make it past the finish line. Despite this defeat, United recovered and went unbeaten in the league for the rest of the calender year, with Robson adding another goal to his tally in a 2-1 victory over West Ham, when he scored after latching on to a back heal from a seventeen-year-old Ryan Giggs. Then, United's imperious captain started to get injured.

On New Year's Day 1992 Manchester United endured an embarrassing and crushing 4-1 defeat to Queen's Park Ranger's without the presence of their captain Bryan Robson. Manchester United manager Alex Ferguson had just been awarded the manager of the month award before kick-off. Going off the form books this surely had to be a one-off and not another domestic capitulation without their skipper in the side.

United made a brief recovery after beating title rivals Leeds United in both the F.A. Cup and the League Cup, either side of a league victory over Everton. However, the unthinkable started to happen. In their next 13 league fixtures the Reds only managed to muster four victories. On each of those four occasions Bryan Robson played in the winning team, yet without him United seemed lacklustre and bereft of ideas. Fergie's men then managed to win a two-legged semi-final in the League Cup against Middlesbrough, with the captain leading the team in both games in a 2-1 aggregate victory. Yet his intermittent appearances coincided with United's poor league form.

Manchester United put their league campaign to one side as they won the League Cup without their injured captain on April 12th 1992 after a 1-0 win over Nottingham Forest, with Brian McClair scoring the only goal of the game. This was the first time the Reds had won a trophy without Bryan Robson in the team since 1977, with Steve Bruce lifting the cup as captain and Andrei Kanchelskis wearing the number seven shirt.

United's extraordinary fixture pile-up meant they then had to play four league games in a week without Robson, who was still absent through injury. After only winning one of these games, United had a win or bust match at Anfield against Liverpool where Robson returned to the side after recovering from injury. The Reds lost 2-0 on the day, and the league title went with it. Moreover they looked like a beaten side from the get-go as the collapse in league form had left a team of broken men. Too many dropped points and failures to score was the theme of the last third of the season. With the accumulation of his age and his track record of injuries, this appeared to be Bryan Robson's last chance at ever winning the league title with Manchester United. Yet Leeds United were crowned the last ever champions of the First Division and a new era was about to start, as the Premier League would now be instated the following season.

Heading into the 1992/1993 season Manchester United were clearly in need of a new young goalscorer and a long term successor to Bryan Robson. The United captain remained just as inspirational as ever, yet he would be 36 this season and his days of lung-busting, box-to-box combat for ninety minutes every week were now surely behind him. Alex Ferguson brought in Dion Dublin from Cambridge United, however, after a shockingly bad start to the Premier League campaign, with two defeats and a draw in their first three matches, Dublin then broke his leg in only his second start for the Reds, after scoring on his full debut the week before.

Robson's first start of the season resulted in a 1-0 defeat to Aston Villa. This came at the end of a twelve game winless streak for United, which saw them crash out of the UEFA Cup, the League Cup and slip way of the pace in the Premier League. However, the captain started United's next three games, all of which they won. This resurgence helped the Reds kick-start their campaign, yet it was the last of these three games that saw a seismic deviation in the chronology of Manchester United's season and indeed, their history. In the Manchester Derby at Old Trafford on December 6th 1992, Bryan Robson left the field at half time and made way for their latest signing, Eric Cantona. The French forward entered the field wearing the number 12 shirt, yet for the foreseeable matches he made the number seven shirt his own.

Steve Bruce was also installed as the regular captain for the remainder of the season due to Robson's limited appearances, although he was still regarded as the captain of the club and remained a prominent influence in the dressing room. United then made a late rally in the title run-in by winning their remaining seven matches, meaning they were crowned as Champions after 26 long years. Robson still had an influence on this winning run by appearing as a substitute in all of these matches. The legendary midfielder then lifted the trophy together with Steve Bruce at Old Trafford after a 3-1 victory over Blackburn Rovers at Old Trafford on May 3rd 1993. If this happened to be Robson's last game for United, then it would be the most fitting way to end his career, as he lapped the pitch holding the trophy with a doting Sir Matt Busby watching from the stands. Yet true to his character, six days later Robson started in the final game of the season away to Wimbledon, wearing the consecrated number seven shirt. The captain was also the only outfield player with a medal not to score that season.

If there was ever a case study into the actualisation of the magic that surrounded the number seven shirt, then it was this day in London. Manchester United were now champions after over a quarter of a century and there was a smouldering atmosphere inside a compact Selhurst Park, with the travelling fans overwhelming the terraces in a more than capacity crowd. The United fans, who outnumbered the home support that day, implored their hero to get on the score sheet, in what would be Bryan Robson's last ever appearance in the number seven jersey of Manchester United.

After months without wearing the shirt that he once made his own, the United captain put on another herculean display which saw him defy his age and injury record, defy his lack of match practice and defy all the odds. It was this day where a transition was made from the player promoting the number seven shirt, to the shirt now enkindling the player. It was as if Robson became aware now of the uniqueness of the numerology behind the number seven shirt of Manchester United. After eighteen months without scoring, the captain was released through on goal, before he composed himself, then slammed the ball into the corner of the net after 72 minutes to give United a 2-0 lead, after Ince had opened the scoring. The game finished 2-1 to the Reds, but the captain had done it, he had made sure that he had the final word on an epic Premier League winning season by getting on the score sheet. His influence was still alive and well, and once again he had achieved what seemed a footballing improbability once more.

The 1993/1994 season saw United entered into the qualifying stages of the Champions League and also the introduction of squad numbers, which meant that the players had to keep the same numbered shirt throughout the whole season. The new campaign saw Robson appear in the Charity Shield as a substitute wearing the number twelve shirt, with the midfielder netting what turned out to be the winning kick in a penalty shoot-out after the game had finished 1-1. He then scored on the opening day of the Premier League season against Norwich City in a 2-0 win, with the United veteran still proving his worth to the squad at the age of 36. Robson enjoyed one of his best runs in the team for several years, despite the summer signing of fellow midfielder Roy Keane, who was billed to be his successor. The foreigner rule, which still applied in the Champions League, also meant the experienced Englishman would be a valuable commodity in this season's European campaign.

After United breezed past Honved in the fist round of the

Champion's League qualifiers, they then had to play Turkish champions Galatasaray. The first leg was at Old Trafford on October 20th 1993 and England's representatives could not have got off to a better start when the ball broke to Robson on the edge of the box after 3 minutes. The United general, who had scored on every big occasion in his illustrious career, turned towards goal with a neat flick between his legs, then slid the ball over the on-rushing keeper. Robson, who was captain for the day, still showed the same desire and fighting spirit that shone through-out his illustrious career. United's new number seven Eric Cantona brought a je-ne-sais-quoi from the continent, yet it was Bryan Robson who was still providing his tour-de-force on the stages of European grandiosity. The game, however, ended 3-3, and after drawing 0-0 in an intimidating match in Turkey, the Reds exited the Champion League before the group stages.

Robson still remained an important part of United's squad, who were romping away with the league title as things stood. Yet at the turn of the year Robson made his last start for three months against Portsmouth in the fifth round of the League Cup. During this time, United lost to Aston Villa in the League Cup final at Wembley at the end of March, before Robson was reintroduced to the line-up in the F.A. Cup semi-final replay, against Oldham Athletic at Maine Road on April 10th 1994. In the first match at Wembley three days earlier, Robson appeared as a substitute when the champions left it late to salvage a replay, with Mark Hughes volleying home in the last minute of extra time, after Neil Pointon gave Oldham the lead. The second match was plain-sailing for the Reds as they finished the game 4-1 winners, with Robson scoring United's third goal in the 62nd minute, after he bundled home a Ryan Giggs corner.

This was a momentous feat for the Old Trafford hero, as he had now incredibly scored in the last four F.A. Cup semi-finals that Manchester United had been involved in. This was the last of Bryan Robson's 99 goals for the club and it was a fitting way to score for the final time. The United legend then led out the team as captain before the final game of the season at home to Coventry City on May 8th 1994. United had already been confirmed as champions a week earlier and towards the end of this match, there became a melancholic and ambivalent atmosphere. The fans knew that after their inspirational leader would once again lift the Premier League trophy with Steve Bruce, he would then have to say goodbye.

The United captain then received a standing ovation in the middle of the pitch before walking off the hallowed grass that he had dominated for so long. His inspiration, his courage, his will and desire to win would be sorely missed, yet as with all good things, they have to come to an end one day. Even when he relinquished his shirt to Eric Cantona, the afterglow of his tenure as the shirt-holder still spilled into his final two seasons without it. Six days later he watched from the sidelines at Wembley, as Manchester United achieved their first ever league and cup double. He had left the club on a high, leading them valiantly for thirteen years before seeing them head back to the summit of English football. The club which he had almost single-handedly dragged to success over the previous decade, had now become a team that could achieve anything.

In all he made 461 appearances for the Reds, scoring 99 goals in the process. He won three F.A. Cup medals, two Premier League medals, a European Cup Winners' Cup medal and a European Super Cup medal. Including replays, he scored in two F.A. Cup finals and five F.A. Cup semi-finals. He is the only player alongside Bobby Charlton, Denis Law, David Herd and Mark Hughes to score in all three of the old formats of European competition and he is Manchester United's longest ever serving club captain. A true legend of the number seven.

ERIC CANTONA

A Saviour From Afar

When Manchester United's wait for the league title stretched to 26 years in 1992, many felt that English football's Holy Grail was a step too far for Alex Ferguson's men. Having capitulated in that season's run-in and allowing Leeds United to snatch the last ever Division One title from right under their noses, it was evident that the Reds were not quite ready to be champions. It was hard to pinpoint exactly what United needed to sit on the coveted perch that Liverpool had their talons on for so long. After all, Fergie's men had won the F.A. Cup, The European Cup Winner's Cup and the League Cup in the previous three years.

Towards the back end of the 1991/1992 season, goals had severely started to dry up. The Reds clearly needed a proven goal scorer if they were to win the inaugural Premier League and so Ferguson swooped for Dion Dublin of Cambridge United. As fate would have it, Dublin broke his leg on his full Old Trafford debut against Crystal Palace in a horror tackle that would rule him out for the season. This meant that the manager had to find himself a new talisman if his Premier League ambitions were to be fulfilled.

United made inquiries about David Hirst of Sheffield Wednesday and Dean Holdsworth of Wimbledon, however, neither deal came to fruition and the quest for a new striker continued for Ferguson. Then by chance, a phone call from Howard Wilkinson, the manager of reigning champions Leeds United, would inadvertently spark the biggest love affair between a player and the fans at the Theatre of Dreams. Wilkinson rang the United boss to inquire about Denis Irwin. After Fergie immediately refused any proposed bid for United's 'Mr Reliable', he then threw the name of Eric Cantona into the conversation. A then knightless Alex Ferguson had famously overheard Gary Pallister and Steve Bruce raving about the enigmatic Frenchman whilst having a post-match bath after playing against Leeds United two months before; and Fergie saw this serendipitous phone call as an opportunity to make one of football's most audacious transfer bids.

On November 26th 1992 Manchester United shocked the footballing world by signing Eric Cantona. Not only had Fergie landed the best player from the previous season's league title winners, he had also got him for a meagre £1.2 million. There were also eyebrows raised about taking on someone who was perhaps the most temperamental footballer of his generation. During his playing days in France, Cantona had been involved in several bust-ups with his team mates and he was also banned for throwing a ball at a referee, in protest at a bad decision.

Cantona had to wait until December 6th 1993 to make his debut, when he replaced Bryan Robson at half time in the Manchester Derby. United won 2-1 with goals from Mark Hughes and Paul Ince, however, it was the Reds' number twelve that day that had everyone talking. The man who was bought to play as a centre forward revolutionised the way Manchester United played all over the pitch. That day, Cantona was seen spraying 50 yard passes from the left back position out to the right wing. If he did not receive the ball up front, he would run back into his own half to find it and then set off an attack which he would attempt to finish. It was revolutionary, it was forward-thinking and it had never been seen before. Manchester United were still waiting for a saviour to lead them out of the football wilderness after 26 years, but was Eric Cantona the one? Many fans believed he was; others just lived in hope.

A week later Eric Cantona wore the iconic number seven shirt for the first time on his full debut against Norwich, then in his next three matches he scored four goals in three games. His first was an equalising goal away to Chelsea in a 1-1 draw on December 19th 1992. He then scored a brace on Boxing Day in a thrilling 3-3 draw with Sheffield Wednesday, where the Reds had to come back from 3-0 down. It was evident that the man from Marseille did not flatter to deceive, as for the first time all season goals started to flow for United. However, it was largely felt that United still needed that extra spark to finally become England 's elite club once more.

On January 9th 1993 when Manchester United played Tottenham Hotspur, Eric Cantona turned football into an art form. Not being satisfied with United playing their best football of the season, the Frenchman decided to take it up a notch. Manchester United won 4-1 with Cantona netting the first goal, yet the second was sheer poetry in motion. Denis Irwin received the ball on the left of the United box, before passing it to Eric Cantona, then as Irwin continued his run, Eric Cantona waved his majestic right boot. Suddenly, with a flash of inspiration that was usually reserved for the stroke of Da Vinci's brush, an epiphany from Socrates or a note from Chopin, Eric Cantona produced the pass of the century which bamboozled the Spurs defence and landed on the chest of Denis Irwin, who then finished the move by scoring.

It had happened; this was the eureka moment that all Manchester United fans had been waiting for. Night became day, dark became light, the clouds had parted and Excalibur had been drawn from its stone. Eric Cantona had the keys to all the locks which kept Manchester United from getting their hands on the league title for over a quarter of a century; but now the king had arrived and every Manchester United fan believed in him.

The Reds still had a lot of work to do that season, and on many occasions they found themselves behind in matches. During the previous season's run-in Sir Alex Ferguson's team found it difficult to produce a diamond moment amongst the rough and tumble of the home straight. This time they had a shining light they could turn to in moments of adversity. On the 35th Anniversary of the Munich Air Disaster, Cantona scored the winner against Sheffield United at Old Trafford in a 2-1 scoreline after the Reds were one-nil down. Then a week later he netted another in a 3-0 victory at home to Middlesbrough. His scoring run continued on March 20th 1993, in Cantona's second Manchester Derby, when he headed in a late equaliser to keep the Red's title hopes alive. United then won five of their next six games, where Eric scored in a momentum changing 3-1 win over table-toppers Norwich City at Carrow Road, before sealing a 3-0 victory over Chelsea at Old Trafford. This run also included a 2-1 win against Sheffield Wednesday, which perhaps spawned the phrase 'Fergie Time' when Bruce headed a 97th minute winner. However, this was now Cantona's time and United ended up winning the league by ten points, whilst playing a brand of football that befitted any team worthy of being champions.

Ferguson's master-stroke signing had paid-off. He spotted the final piece of the Manchester United jigsaw and when it fell into place, the spirit of Manchester United had finally arisen to help them conquer their homeland once more.

The Genius Rebels

They say there is a fine line between genius and madness. We saw the genius of Cantona during United's title winning campaign of 1993, and now we were about to see the equilibrium, with the madness balancing out the complex mind of King Eric. At the start of the 1993/1994 season United began where they had left off; and a blistering start saw them fourteen points clear at the top of the league by the end of November.

Cantona missed United's first four games due to a wrist injury, however, he scored in his return match against Southampton with another goal-of-the-season contender. From twenty five yards out he merely caressed the ball in his stride to chip Tim Flowers from a seemingly impossible angle. After scoring in his next game his genius mind then set a target no one else could see, let alone hit.

When Manchester United played Chelsea at Stamford Bridge on 11th September 1993, Eric Cantona attempted something so audacious that not even his team mates saw it coming. When the ball sat up on the half way line in Cantona's periphery, he saw that Dmitri Kharine was of his line. Then in one pirouette, United's number seven managed to volley the ball over the opposition keeper, only to see his effort bounce up off the bar. Cantona was inches away from creating history, however, perhaps future players may have taken note of this, with attempts from the half way line being no longer outside the boundaries of thought for a Manchester United number seven.

In United's next game he did manage to hit the target against Arsenal at Old Trafford, with a strike that had Ferguson of the bench with a look of astonishment on his face. After being awarded a free-kick from thirty yards out, the rest of United's regular takers turned down the opportunity to have an attempt on goal, as it appeared to be too far out. However, Paul Ince stood over the ball, then teed-up Cantona to have a strike on goal. In a flash the ball was in the top corner of the Stretford End net with Cantona running away, waving his plastered arm in celebration.

The height of Cantona's genius was now on show, so where was the catch? His artist-like flair had been unleashed from one chamber of his football brain. So where were the signs of trouble that usually come with it?

During the 1993-1994 campaign, Manchester United and Eric Cantona started their first Champions League adventure. After breezing through the first qualifying stage against lowly Honved,

United now faced the unfancied Turkish champions Galatasaray. The Reds were held to a thrilling, yet disappointing 3-3 draw at Old Trafford which saw Cantona prod home a late equaliser. United now had to go to the Ali Sami Yen Stadium and win.

The home side knew any draw, except an unlikely repeat of the first leg's score or above, would see them through. After a frustrating night of man-marking and time-wasting tactics, United soon found themselves heading out of the competition. Cantona, however, appeared to become frustrated long before the end. In the 77th minute, Galatasaray seemed in no rush to take a throw-in, which caused Eric Cantona to kick the ball out of the reserve keeper Nezih Ali Bologlu's hands, before knocking him to the ground with an elbow charge. It was possible that the United striker could have saw a red card for that incident alone, but it was left unnoticed by the referee. He was eventually sent-off at the final whistle for what appeared to be a show of dissent towards the Swiss referee Kurt Röthlisberger regarding his performance. As the referee presented Cantona with his first red card as a Manchester United player, the enigmatic Frenchman punched the ball in the air in protest, before he, and several other United players, saw the wrath of a policeman's baton. If the antidote to his genius was kept bottled up inside King Eric, then a trip to what the Turkish fans called 'Hell' saw the top of that bottle start to unscrew.

Four days later on November 7th 1993 the Reds took part in the Manchester Derby at Maine Road. City fans took pleasure in United's elimination from European competition by waving Turkish Delights at the travelling fans, before the home side then revelled in a 2-0 half-time lead. Monsieur Cantona, still clearly fired up by the events in Istanbul, was having not of it and took the game by the scruff of the neck. The commentator that day, Martin Tyler, described Cantona as "Having a baton in his hand and conducting an orchestra" as Eric's influential display saw him score two goals to level the game. After each goal went in, more and more United fans were seen celebrating in the home section, and when Roy Keane made it 3-2 late on, more than half the stadium celebrated showing why United were kings of the city and why Eric Cantona was becoming the leader of his football team.

Manchester United were now cruising along unscathed in both the league and the domestic cup competitions. So long as Cantona was playing at his imperious best and the reigning champions kept the same mentality that saw them over the line in the previous season, then nothing apart from a period of madness could possibly upset the apple cart.

In December Cantona did, however, start to show acts of petulance as he kicked a Norwich City defender in response to a foul. Then in the F.A. Cup fourth round in January, retaliating to another foul, he put his heel into the face of a second Norwich defender. Both incidents went unnoticed by the referees, yet his wizardry on the field was being noticed by everyone.

Soon the Tricolore flags were out in force. Every time Cantona had the ball at his feet there was a clatter of lifting seats throughout Old Trafford as the fans rose in anticipation, which was often followed by a clatter of applause. The crowd fed off his artistry, Cantona fed off the love from the fans. He was serenaded by choruses of 'Ooh Aah Cantona' and his followers were infatuated by his mercurialness. They loved his covert and overindulgent use of the back-heel, his deft flicks and nonchalant touches. These were all looked upon as high risk manoeuvres by many in the English game, but nonetheless they could alter the tempo and pattern of any football match. His up-turned collar was mirrored by the fans who wore his replica shirt. It became a symbol of reverence and a statement of love.

Despite the European blip, the rest of the season was going according to plan and Cantona continued to shine during the grey clouds and sodden pitches of the winter months. His brilliance on the football pitch could brighten up even the dullest of football matches, but at a cold, muddy Selhurst Park in February against Wimbledon, this would take some doing. Eric rose to the challenge and after a long searching ball from Denis Irwin was half-cleared by the Dons' defence, Cantona took one touch in his stride, to set up a dipping volley from the edge of the box that crashed in off the crossbar. Cantona's love affair with the F.A. Cup continued and he saved this day for one of his greatest ever United goals. However, history would go on to prove that Selhurst Park would become a ground of mixed emotions.

As Manchester United entered the business end of the season, they entered a period which was to be dubbed 'Mad March' – and Eric Cantona would once again be very much involved in this madness.

In his French playing days, Cantona was dropped from the French national team due to 'poor form'. His retort was to call his manager Henri Michel 'un sac a merde' meaning a 'shit bag' during a televised interview. He subsequently received a one year ban from international football. This ban was later rescinded when Michel Platini took over as the national coach. Then on May 15th 1990 whilst playing for Marseille he threw a ball at a referee after disagreeing with a decision made against him. This earned him a month suspension; however, his punishment was doubled after calling each member of the disciplinary committee an idiot to their face. After this incident he decided to quit football altogether. However, his route back into English football seemed to have given him a new lease of life and the perfect stage for a man of such complexity. The man who had sought haven at Auxerre, Marseille, Martigues, Bordeaux, Montpellier, Nimes and Leeds all in the space of seven years appeared to have finally found contentment. However towards the end of the 1993-1994 season, the yin which was Cantona's genius was now about to show how much it was dependent on the yang which was his madness.

On March 19th 1994 he was sent off for stamping on the chest of Swindon Town defender John Moncur after a tussle on the pitch. Then four days later he saw red for two bookable offences against Arsenal. This was sandwiched between a defeat to Chelsea in the league, a Peter Schmeichel sending-off in the quarter-final of the F.A. Cup and a 3-1 loss to Aston Villa in the final of the League Cup, where this time it was Andrei Kanchelskis who saw red for a deliberate handball. United managed to end the month of March on a high with victory over Liverpool at Old Trafford, however, playing with ten men in four matches during that month took its toll, as their lead at the top of the league had been cut to just three points. Their dreams of a domestic treble evaporated after a disappointing performance at Wembley; which saw Les Sealey playing goal instead of the suspended Peter Schmeichel and more significantly, the Reds now had to play important matches without the suspended Cantona, which included an F.A. Cup semi-final tie against Oldham Athletic, and a potential Premier League decider against Kenny Dalglish's Blackburn Rovers.

Cantona received a three match ban for violent conduct in the match against Swindon, which was accepted by the club, yet it was generally thought that he was unlucky to receive his marching orders at Highbury. Consequently the rules had to apply and he received a five match ban for his misdemeanours, which would see Cantona missing a large chunk of the title run-in. During the final matches of the previous year, United's number seven brought an element of calmness and control to a side who had previously crumbled on the home-straight. This time they were already starting to teeter, and for the next five games, his presence would be gone.

Eric Cantona was now the most exciting footballer in English football. This coupled with his temperamental personality, his rebellious nature and his passion for the arts made him the most talked about player in the land. The paradox that he was voted players' player of the year whist under suspension summed the United striker up perfectly. For one who loved poetry so much, this unprecedented feat was the perfect metaphor for Eric Cantona's football career.

His absence in the team showed when first they lost 2-0 to Blackburn Rovers, who were now level-pegging with United at the top of the league, before a 1-0 defeat to Wimbledon compounded their misery. Their lack of cutting edge was reminiscent of the title run-in of 1992, where a moment of class was needed to make the difference amongst the pressure, the fixture pile-ups and the mind games. In between these two defeats were two F.A. Cup semi-final matches against Oldham Athletic. Again, United were struggling to find a path to goal, and with a minute of extra time remaining at Wembley the Reds were trailing 1-0. It took a last gasp goal from Mark Hughes to salvage a replay, which was a telling event on two counts. First of all it kept United's dream of their first double alive, secondly it meant that an extra fixture had to be added during Cantona's ban. This allowed him to return to league action a game earlier, which turned out to be the Manchester Derby.

Upon his return the United number seven scored twice in a 2-0 win, with the first goal having a hallmark of genius about it. A long searching ball by Andrei Kanchelskis was taken down by Cantona on his heal, then in the same motion he finished clinically with his other foot. It was clear that the Frenchman was sorely missed in the previous five games, as United won their next four games upon his return. The Reds' second Premier League success in a row was completed after Blackburn Rovers lost to Coventry City with two games remaining. Now United had the chance to win their first ever Double when they faced Chelsea in the 1994 F.A Cup final.

United had lost twice already to Chelsea this season, with both games ending 1-0 to the London side. Gavin Peacock scored the winner in both games, but it was the first match at Stamford Bridge that hit the headlines for the Reds when Eric Cantona memorably hit the crossbar from the half-way line.

In Cantona's first F.A Cup final, United were outplayed by Chelsea in a first half of football which saw their own crossbar rattled early on, ironically by Gavin Peacock; and after the Chelsea striker had already sunk United twice in the league that season, the signs looked ominous for the Reds. United upped their game in the second half and were awarded a penalty an hour into the match. Cantona, after having a bet on the pitch with Denis Wise that he would score, casually put the ball on the spot and sent Dmitri Kharine the wrong way to put the champions in front. Six minutes later they were awarded another spot kick; same player, same corner, same result. United went on to win the game 4-0 with further goals from Hughes and McClair, which meant that they were crowned as double winners for the first time in their history.

On the bus on the way back to Manchester, Cantona gave a rare televised interview. When he was asked about the two penalties that he scored, he simply said "If he dives to the right, I score to the left. If he dives to the left, I score to the right."

In the 1993/1994 season, Eric became the first non-British winner of the Professional Footballers' Association's Player of the Year Award. But the other Cantona was also on view - as the first man to win the award while banned from playing the game. While his Manchester United team mates were challenging for the honours in the season's climactic games, Cantona was sitting out a suspension for violent conduct on the pitch.

As the new season approached, it was widely accepted that Sir Alex Ferguson was willing to accept Cantona's volatile behaviour, on the basis that curbing his temperament may take away the genius that wins football matches. With United aspiring to win a third Premier League trophy in a row, they knew that the rebellious Fenchman had to be available for as many games as he could, as missing games through suspension almost cost United the title in the previous season.

Starting as you mean to go on was perhaps not a phrase translatable in French as Cantona was involved in controversy before the 1994/1995 campaign had even started. On August 6th 1994 during a pre-season friendly against Rangers, the P.F.A. Player of the Year was sent off for a dangerous lunge on Stephen Crossley, only a minute after receiving a yellow card for dissent.

United's talisman missed the opening three games of the season for his troubles, however, the rest of the team started the season well with seven points from their opening three games. Cantona once again scored on his return match as he netted the opening goal in a three-nil win at home to Wimbledon.

Despite seeing the red mist before the season had even started, Eric Cantona and Manchester United were going well in the league with Cantona regularly on the score sheet, scoring five times in his next eight matches. This included a goal against former club Leeds United from the penalty spot in a 2-1 defeat and a goal in a 3-2 loss to Ipswich Town two weeks later. After a winning penalty against West Ham United at Old Trafford in a 1-0 win, he then scored from the spot in a 4-2 victory over title rivals Blackburn Rovers. Then on November 10th 1994, a goal in United's 5-0 destruction of Manchester City meant Cantona had now scored in four Manchester Derbies in a row. The United striker had netted ten times before Christmas in all; and at the turn of the year it seemed that last season's top scorer was heading down the same path.

In the F.A. Cup third round in January, United commenced their defence of the trophy against Sheffield United at Bramall Lane. After Mark Hughes broke the deadlock, Cantona received the ball twenty-five yards from goal. He then nonchalantly chipped the ball over the keeper and into the net via the crossbar. It was another moment of sheer genius from the United rebel. He saw a picture before anyone else could see it, creating another masterpiece which left onlookers astounded and his teammates elated. Manchester United then faced title rivals Blackburn Rovers at Old Trafford in the most important match of the season so far. Cantona again grabbed the headlines by heading home the winner ten minutes from time. It was evident that Cantona's unrivalled flair was again the difference when Manchester United had to fight their way out of a stalemate. We could only guess what would have happened for the rest of the season and if Cantona was going to take centre stage yet again. However, three days later the football world was turned on its head.

United's temperamental number seven had been sent-off four times previously in his Old Trafford career; and on January 25th 1995 against Crystal Palace at Sehurst Park, he made it number five. An on-field tussle with Crystal Palace's Luke Shaw, who could have saw a card several times himself and who's actions on the pitch were going unnoticed by referee Alan Wilkie, resulted in Cantona taking matters into his own hands. After appearing to kick out at Shaw, United's number seven received a red card on the advice of the linesman. After losing it on the pitch, Eric started walking towards the tunnel, where he received a torrent of abuse from the home fans, and in particular, Crystal Palace fan Matthew Simmons. The United kit-man Norman Davies tried to lead the volatile Frenchman to safety, but he broke free of Davies' grasp before jumping over the advertisement hoardings and planting a kung-fu style kick on Simmons' chest. The two then proceeded to exchange blows as stewards tried to tear Cantona away. Peter Schmeichel then lead the Frenchman back towards the tunnel amidst a shower of tea cups being hurled by the home fans.

The events that unfolded at Selhurst Park were seen on the front page of every tabloid newspaper the next day. Soon everyone, including those not even involved in football, founded themselves casting their opinions on the incident.

As a result Manchester United banned the Frenchman until the end of the season and fined him £20,000. The ban was later extended by the Football Association until September 30th 1995. The United striker also faced legal proceedings and Cantona was arrested and convicted of assault, resulting in a two-week prison sentence. This was later overturned in the appeal court and instead he was sentenced to 120 hours of community service.

With the man being a self-confessed lover of philosophy, Cantona had his own view of events, following the media circus surrounding his eight month ban for a Kung-Fu kick on a football supporter. Having felt aggrieved at the amount of press coverage and scrutiny he had received following the Selhurst Park incident and the severity of the ban from the F.A., Eric Cantona plotted his chance to turn the tables on all of his adversaries. The King once again became a martyr for United's cause by making a stand against his and the club's long standing battle against the powers-that-be, by quoting: "When the seagulls follow the trawler, it is because they think that sardines will be thrown into the sea." In front of a bemused audience, these were Cantona's parting words as he left to take his punishment from the F.A.

After his ban was lengthened to eight months United boss Ferguson claimed; "I don't think any player in the history of football will get what he got - unless they had killed Bert Millichip's dog." This was a retort at then F.A. chairman Bert Millichip who deemed the initial ban made by the club to be too lenient.

In the absence of Cantona, Fergie's men went on to lose the league on the final day of the season, after failing to beat West Ham United. Then a week later, they lost in the F.A. Cup final to Everton. Their pursuit of another double was quashed in the final week of the season, however, many believed that Cantona's presence would have seen them over the line easily in both competitions; and that United's season was effectively over the moment Cantona kicked the Crystal Palace fan.

During in the summer, it seemed inevitable that Eric Cantona would leave English football for good. In a desperate act, Ferguson travelled to Paris in attempt to persuade Cantona to stay at Old Trafford. In order to avoid any press intrusion, Fergie resorted to receiving a lift by a trustworthy associate of Cantona, on the back of a motorbike. This was another legendary fable in the chronicles of Cantona's journey in English football. The boss sat in Eric Cantona's hotel room where he made an appeal to his striker to stay at Manchester United. A man who had made many motivational and heart-rending speeches must have used his greatest ever rhetoric on this occasion, as he managed to talk Eric into staying at Manchester United.

This pursuit of Cantona in France showed that a then knightless

Alex Ferguson would be willing to accept Cantona's rebellious side, the media circus around him and his volatile nature. The acceptance that genius is often complemented by madness encouraged him to fight for his most prized possession.

With Eric Cantona, and like many geniuses in any trade, they know no boundaries, just endless horizons. This lack of boundaries allowed Eric Cantona to produce a brand football that had seldom been seen before, because his mind did not allow him to have any limitations with a football. Yet what came with this was no limit on his anger. When a normal footballer's mind would tell them to stop attempting an impossible back-heel, Cantona's mind would allow him to do it. However, on the flip side, a normal footballer would decline from attacking a member of the crowd, because they are aware that they have certain role in setting an example. They know they are in the spotlight and thus they have to portray a heightened manner of social decorum. Cantona has no mechanism to prevent this. A genius mind knows no limits of any kind.

The Return of The King

At the start of the 1995/1996 season the focus was turned away from Cantona momentarily, as the Reds were beaten 3-1 by Aston Villa in that legendary game on the opening day of the season, where United fielded a team mainly comprised of youth products. After selling Paul Ince, Mark Hughes and Andrei Kanchelskis, Manchester United seemed short on flair and experience, however, what many fans and famously pundits forgot to realise, is that United's most inspirational player from the previous two-and-a-half seasons was scheduled to return to the first team against Liverpool on October 1st. The day Manchester United fans were calling the 'Red October'.

Despite Alex Ferguson's naysayers, United remained unbeaten in the next six matches leading up to Eric Cantona's return, winning five of them in the process. The return of the enigmatic Frenchman was expected to re-establish the Red's cutting edge that saw them almost win the domestic treble in 1994. United's young players had proved that they were no longer pretenders to the thrones left by the departed senior players, yet there was still only one king, and his long awaited return was finally here.

Cantona was named in United's starting eleven for the first match he was eligible to play in, after his lengthy ban. Many eyebrows were raised at this decision, as nine months without first team football in the cut-and-thrust of the Premier League seemed like a tall order for any player, but when it came to tall orders, Cantona stood head and shoulders above the rest.

As the fans anticipated his return to the field, Old Trafford was awash with the French national flag. The stands were adorned with images of Cantona's face. Fans who were wearing their number seven shirts turned up their collars, like the raising of a flag upon the presence of royalty. Their chins were no longer half-mast, instead they stood tall and proud. As the players emerged from the tunnel, a collective breath was drawn from the crowd, and then a joyous cheer was let out, as bringing up the rear of his troops was their idol. With his imperious posture, chest puffed out, back straight and head held high, Eric Cantona had re-appeared from the football wilderness. The king had returned.

Inevitably, Cantona had an immediate impact on his return to Premier League football. In a pulsating 2-2 draw at Old Trafford against the old enemy, he set up United's opener after only two minutes, with a floaty cross-goal pass which was converted by Nicky Butt. The Reds then fell behind through two goals from Robbie Fowler, and in United's quest for an equaliser, Ryan Giggs earned United a penalty with twenty minutes to go. So now the stage was set, as King Eric strutted up to the penalty spot without a hint of apprehension. Like a sculpted philosopher, he stood there cold-eyed with his hands on hips for a couple of seconds, sucking the energy from the crowd, basking in the glory that all eyes were on him. He then nonchalantly scored the inevitable equaliser by sending the goalkeeper the wrong way. He then duly celebrated with the United fans, by spinning around the stanchion behind the goal. Cantona had rescued a point for United in what would prove to be a season to remember, but more importantly - Eric Cantona was back.

On his return match he was clearly running on pure adrenalin, and it was perhaps his lack of match fitness that saw the Frenchman go eight matches before his next goal, which was also from the penalty spot in a 1-1 draw with Nottingham Forest on November 27th 1995 United then went on a run of only two wins in nine games, which lead to table toppers Newcastle United opening up a seemingly unassailable twelve point lead heading into January.

If everyone involved in football thought they had seen it all from Eric Cantona, then they were seriously mistaken. The next chapter of his career at Manchester United must have taken even the most romantic of script-writers by surprise.

On January 22nd 1996 United faced a West Ham side who had frustrated the Reds at Upton Park in the two previous seasons, with the second occasion famously stopping Fergie's men from winning the league in 1995. On this occasion Eric Cantona opened the scoring for United after eight minutes and despite some rocky moments they hung-on to win the game 1-0, with Cantona being the only scorer. The Reds had achieved their first league win of the calendar year and the score-line and goal-scorer would prove to be ominous for the rest of the league.

After scoring in the FA Cup against Reading, Cantona then returned to Selhurst Park for the first time since his infamous stamp on a Crystal Palace fan. This time the opposition was Wimbledon and inevitably Cantona was on the score sheet. In a 4-2 win over the Dons, the United number seven netted twice and after his first goal Cantona ran into the crowd again. This time it was to celebrate with the home fans, this time it was for all the right reasons.

Before the Reds faced Newcastle United at St James's Park on March 4th 1996, the title run-in had started to take shape. United had whittled Newcastle's lead at the top from 12 points in December to just 4 points going into March. With United winning their previous five league games, the Magpies looked at this fixture as the one that would kill off any lingering title hopes for the Red Devils. After stern resistance from the United back four and a wonder show by Peter Schmeichel, Fergie's men somehow kept the game scoreless at the break. United knew that with Eric on the pitch anything could happen and early in the second half he latched on to a Phil Neville cross to put the Reds one-nil in front. United held on for the win and severely damaged Newcastle's title chances.

Cantona then scored in six of the next seven games. The first being a last-gasp injury time equaliser against Queens Park Rangers in a 1-1 draw at Loftus Road. This match occurred amid a sequence of 1-0 wins.

When United played Arsenal at Old Trafford on 20th March 1996, they were once again looking for a flash of brilliance to break the deadlock. Then on 66 minutes Cantona scored the winner when he thundered in a twenty-five yard volley off the crossbar. Four days later the mercurial Frenchman scored the only goal against Tottenham Hotspur after a piece of individual brilliance saw him weave past the Spurs defence before slotting the ball into the bottom corner of the net. After United progressed past Chelsea in the semi-final of the F.A. Cup with a 2-1 win, Cantona converted a penalty in United's next match after leaving it late to beat Manchester City 3-2 at Maine Road. Then two days later, he hit the winner against Coventry City at Old Trafford in another 1-0 win.

The Reds were now level on points with Newcastle United causing their manager Kevin Keegan to have a televised public meltdown, saying he would "love it" if he beat United to the title.

United still had some work to do as they needed four points from their remaining two games to reclaim the Premier League trophy. In the penultimate league game of the season, they breezed past Nottingham Forest with a 5-0 win, with Cantona scoring the fifth goal a minute from time. After he scored, he kissed his hand and spun to all corners of the stadium before falling to the ground. Cantona was in love with football again and he wanted to share this love with his adoring fans. The Reds were then crowned as champions with a 3-0 win at Middlesbrough.

1996 was another vintage year for Manchester United and it was no coincidence that it coincided with Eric Cantona's most influential season. In the title run-in, King Eric scored a string of vital match-winning goals in a series of one-nil results, which led to United's third Premier League trophy in four years.

Eric Cantona was a footballing contradiction. He did not need friends; he did not need to be loved. But the love he felt from the Manchester United fans during the dark days of his total football ban inspired him to create his next masterpiece. Instead of packing his bindle and walking away forever, the troubled Frenchman cleaned the hard soil from his boots like Cezanne would clean the hard paint off his brushes. His lifeless, limp number seven shirt which lay desolate with a down-turned collar, like the discarded canvas of a failed artist, would soon be pinned back to the easel. Upon his return United raised their game just as Cantona's collar rose like Lazarus. The man that defied convention would now see this defiance rub-off on his young teammates who were told they could not win anything. The rebel without a cause now had a cause, and so did the rest of the players, as the fresh-faced team which were deemed too inexperienced would now go down in history as the Champions of England. Fittingly, in the absence of the injured Steve Bruce, it was the returning Cantona who lifted the trophy as captain.

However, Cantona wasn't finished there as the prospect of another double, to go with the one they won two years previous, was on the horizon. The United number seven was again captain for the day and as he lead out his troops, there was optimistic hope that the perennial match-winner could wave his magic wand one more time. In a rare dull game between the two North-West rivals, time began to run out. With extra-time on the horizon and the score at 0-0, United found themselves in a familiar position to matches in the league campaign, with Cantona so often the saviour on those occasions. This match though seemed a game too far for Fergie's men as United looked jaded after a long, emotional season. Yet Eric Cantona, rebellious as he is, did not read from the same script as everyone else.

With five minutes to go, United won a corner right in front of their own fans. As Beckham swung the ball in from the right, Liverpool goalkeeper David James flapped at the cross, leaving the ball to break in Cantona's direction. Most players would have taken a touch as the ball seemed to bounce behind him. However, with James off his line and from an awkward and seemingly impossible angle, the United striker somehow wrapped his majestic right boot around the ball and kept it low enough for the ball to sail through a crowded box and into the goal.

Cantona had not only dug out a contortionist style strike to seal the first ever 'Double Double' for the Reds, he also dug his team out of a hole for the umpteenth time that season with a moment of genius that only Eric Cantona could produce. It was an eye-defying climax to Eric Cantona's return season after his ban. He showed his importance in the title run-in when Manchester United needed a flash of inspiration to gain points in a heavy fixture schedule. The spark of genius, that was missing in the home-straights of the 1992 and 1995 seasons, was back to drag his team mates over the line. To this day it remains footballs most unimaginable comeback story for any player. If United's Premier League dominance appeared to go up in smoke, then Eric Cantona was the phoenix that rose from the ashes. The 1995/1996 season was a blank canvas for art-lover Eric; and just as Rembrandt painted the Return of the Prodigal Son, a picture depicting forgiveness mixed with judgement, United's own returning prodigy basked in the glory of his forgiving fans, repaying them with a second double in three years, whilst silencing the judgement that exuded from the rest of the football world.

Au Revoir Cantona

Unlike the rest of Manchester United's famous five who wore the sacred jersey, Cantona finished his playing days at Old Trafford. The United number seven was also now officially the club captain, following the departure of Steve Bruce in the summer. The 1996/1997 season started well for the United captain, after scoring the opening goal in the Charity Shield upon his return to Wembley and scoring against Wimbledon on the opening day of the season. Selhurst Park would always be a bitter-sweet arena for the United striker, after his infamous stamp on a Crystal Palace fan. Yet once again the number seven sought reprieve by netting another goal at the scene of the crime. He then found redemption against Leeds United at Ellend Road on September 7th 1996, where after missing the first penalty of his Manchester United career, the Frenchman then scored United's fourth goal in a 4-0 win over his former club. Then after netting a double against Nottingham Forest a week later, he notched two Champions League goals against Fenerbahce in October and then Rapid Vienna in December.

The striker then lit up Old Trafford when United played Sunderland on December 21st 1996 with a goal that summed up the United legend's career. After a quiet start to the season by his own standards, Cantona took the ball on half-way and bamboozled two Sunderland players before playing a one-two with Brian McClair. With defenders trailing in his wake and the goalkeeper approaching, United's football genius chipped the ball from the edge of the box onto the angle of the post and into the net. When most players would do a lap of honour after scoring such a goal, his nonchalant celebration said it all when he just looked around at the adoring fans with his arms aloft, as if to say "Well, what do you expect?".

In the final game of 1996 United were awarded a penalty against Leeds United at Old Trafford, which Cantona scored to put United top of the league, whilst rectifying his miss against the Yorkshire club back in September. He then netted a late winner against Southampton on February 1st 1997 in a 2-1 win which kept United's title charge on course. Eric then put his mark on the Champions League, with United's first venture into the knockout stages of the new format. A superb strike against Porto in the first leg of the quarter-final helped United to a 4-0 win at Old Trafford, before they progressed to the last four with a goalless draw in Portugal. He then scored in three successive league matches, starting with a goal against Eveton in a 2-0 win at Goodison Park, then a consolation strike in a 3-2 loss to Derby County at home. Cantona then scored what turned out to be his last ever goal in a Manchester United shirt, when he turned in an Andy Cole cross in a 3-2 win over Blackburn Rovers at Ewood Park. This came after the United striker had seen his penalty saved by Tim Flowers earlier in the match. United then went on to win the Premier League title for the fourth time in five years, with captain and number seven Eric Cantona lifting the trophy.

He came to Old Trafford. He saw a vision that no one else could, then he conquered. It was a match made in heaven for a player who was lost in the desert looking for the oasis, until eventually the oasis came to him. Eric Cantona not only provided the missing spark of inspiration to make Sir Alex Ferguson's Manchester United the greatest team of the nineties, his ingenuity rubbed off on a generation of young players who carried his influence throughout their careers.

His none-conformity to regular mundane football not only helped Manchester United achieve their first league title in 27 years, he also helped the Red Devils win their first ever league and cup double. After his nine month ban he then gave belief to a team who were dubbed 'too young' which helped them win the Premier League and F.A. Cup for the second time. Now they had proved their greatness by retaining the title. Once his work was done he left at the top because he never wanted his magic to fade. We never saw a Cantona that was past his prime, which has kept him immortalised as a genius like a rock star who dies young. The biggest tribute to his legacy is that his name is still chanted by the Old Trafford faithful to this day. Eric Cantona - a legend of the number seven.

DAVID BECKHAM

The Class of '92

After Alex Ferguson's arrival at Old Trafford the manager's main priority was to revamp the youth system at the Club. Manchester United had a number of local trialists attempting to catch the eye of the coaching staff, however, their much improved scouting network saw their eyes searching the breadth of the country for young prospects. This revolution led to United's talent spotters knocking on the door of Leytonstone boy David Beckham, who had drew attention to himself by excelling at the Tottenham Hotspur School of Excellence and being named the Under-15 Player of the Year in 1990 for Brimsdown Rovers' youth team. Manchester United landed the signature of David Beckham on his 14th birthday on May 2nd 1989.

Beckham had to travel from his home town to Manchester in his schoolboy days, yet this was not an unusual event for the Londoner, as his father Ted was an avid Manchester United fan who used to frequently travel to Old Trafford to watch the Reds play. Beckham himself was a Manchester United fan, and Intriguingly he was a mascot for Manchester United in 1986 for a league match against West Ham United.

United's youth team were soon attracting attention from the coaching staff, the senior players and the media. Little did this group of 17 year-olds going into the F.A. Youth Cup in the 1992/1993 season know what a forbearance this would prove to be. United's youth squad were affectionately known as 'Fergie's Fledglings' a name which carried the same connotations as the 'Busby Babes'. During the fifties Manchester United's youth team won the F.A. Youth Cup five times in a row, with many of those players going on to make first team appearances and win Division One winner's medals and caps for their countries.

In the 1992/1993 season, many of the club's staff who associated with this new generation of young players felt that Fergie's Fledglings had the potential to emulate the great players of the Matt Busby era.

As expected the Manchester United youth team got to the final that year, where they historically beat Crystal Palace 6-3 on aggregate over two legs. David Beckham scored in the first leg at Selhurst Park and it was evident that he, along with several other of his teammates that day, were destined to have a chance of first team football at the biggest club in the world.

The players who won the Youth Cup were dubbed the 'Class of '92' and on the back of this, Sir Alex Ferguson saw the 1992/1993 season as the right time to blood his young apprentices into the first team. David Beckham's first chance came on September 23rd 1992 in a League Cup tie against Brighton and Hove Albion, where he made a second-half substitute appearance. In the days that preceded squad numbers, Beckham entered the field wearing the number fourteen shirt, replacing fellow right-winger Andrei Kanchelskis who was wearing the number seven shirt for that match. As history would prevail, this replacement would prove hugely symbolic in more ways than one. This was Beckham's only appearance of the season with the physicality of first team football perhaps too much for a slip of a seventeen year old. However, he did help guide Manchester United to another F.A. Youth Cup final where on this occasion they finished runners-up to Leeds United.

The next season Beckham played much of his football in the

reserve league. Back in the early nineties the reserves were a tough learning curve for many young players as they were up against seasoned professionals who took no mercy. Whereas nowadays the reserves are almost exclusively for youth team development, at the time that Beckham turned professional the reserve league was mainly a pool off first team players returning from injury and players who were dropped with a point to prove. United won the reserve league in 1993/1994 with the class of '92 graduates playing the majority of those games.

On September 21st 1994 Manchester United were scheduled to face Port Vale in the first leg of the League Cup second round. This was a pivotal day in the lives of many young players at Manchester United and elsewhere in the country. The League Cup, which seemed lower down on the list of priorities for the United boss, had now become a tournament to blood his young players into first team action. The game itself carries a momentous amount of iconography for it being the first time that any manager had risked a team full of untried youth team and reserve players for any match. Although this was frowned upon at the time, many, if not all clubs have followed suit with this practise. As far as United were concerned it was another historic day for the club. In a match which will be remembered for Paul Scholes scoring two goals on his debut for the Reds, it was also the match that David Beckham played a starting role for the first time. Sir Alex Ferguson had taken the leap and put faith in all of his talented youngsters. Many of the first team players at the club had to stand up and take note, as Premier League action would not be far away for a teenage Beckham and his fellow youth team mates, with the senior stars knowing their place in the team could soon be tested.

On December 7th 1994 Manchester United faced Galatasaray at Old Trafford in the Champions League. With the foreigner rule restrictions still in place Ferguson decided to field some of his English youngsters against the Turkish champions. After Simon Davies scored the first goal, David Beckham then made it 2-0 with a strike from outside the area. The commentator that day Brian Moore exclaimed "First Davies the youngster, second Beckham the youngster … well, the young boys are doing Alex Ferguson proud" The game ended 4-0, yet despite this, Manchester United were knocked out of Europe after an already qualified IFK Gothenburg side, who needed to beat Barcelona at the Nou Camp, could only draw.

Although the Reds failed to make it past the group stage, there were many positives that could be taken from the game. The 'foreigner rule' had clearly hampered United in the early years of the Champions League, however, they could now take comfort in the fact that they had several English players who proved they could step up to the mark on the European stage. David Beckham put on an impressive display on the right side of midfield in place of Kanchelskis, yet it would seem incomprehensible to suggest that he would replace the 1994/1995 top scorer on this basis alone.

His size was also a concern for the United coaching staff, as despite his talent, he appeared too lightweight for the physicality of the Premier League. With this in mind, he was sent to Preston North End for a short loan spell. On March 4th 1995 David Beckham's fortunes seemed to have taken a turn for the worst: on the same day that Manchester United recorded their biggest ever Premier League victory with a 9-0 win over Ipswich Town, David Beckham was now making his debut for Preston in the lower leagues of English football. Despite this, he made an immediate impact at Deepdale by scoring directly from a corner. Instead of a seeing a young undeveloped player being bullied off the field in the rough and tumble of lower league football, Beckham exhibited the magnificence of his golden right boot. In his next game for Preston he then scored the first free-kick of his career. After bending the ball into the corner off the net with his unique ankle breaking posture, English football could now see that this kid was not just another reserve player at a big club who flattered to deceive, before dropping into the lower tiers of the football league. This was a teenager who was technically head and shoulders above the rest of the division; and after only five matches, Sir Alex Ferguson recalled him back to his Manchester United squad.

On April 2nd 1995 Beckham made his full league debut for Manchester United when he was given a starting role on the right wing for the Reds against Leeds United at Old Trafford. The match ended 0-0 which dented United's title hopes that season, however, the young midfielder wearing the number 24 shirt caught the eye of the fans and the manager, which prompted Sir Alex Ferguson to start him in the next match against Crystal Palace in the F.A. Cup semi-final. United drew 2-2 against Palace before winning the replay 2-0. Yet the 1994/1995 season ended on a forgettable low for Manchester United, after losing the league on the last day of the season by failing to beat West Ham United and the losing in the F.A. Cup final to Everton. However, it was the following summer that had many people involved in football wallowing in even more disbelief.

You Can't Win The League With Kids

Prior to the 1995/1996 season, the lifeblood of Manchester United's most successful era had been the Busby Babes. Sir Matt Busby's vision of turning to youth instead of experience became an ingrained philosophy at the club. During the fifties Busby audaciously replaced a successful, yet ageing team with untried youngsters in a bid to conquer the English First Division and then compete on a European level. Sir Alex Ferguson soon recognised this blue print for success, however, many believed that the Reds current squad were unlucky not to retain the double in 1995, after all, the same team had already won Manchester United's first ever double in 1994. Moreover, Andy Cole would no longer be cup-tied and Eric Cantona was due to return from his ban on October 1st of the upcoming season.

On the-other-hand after failing to retain the title, United's squad appeared to need strengthening due to the spending power of their rivals. The 1995 title winners Blackburn Rovers had spent big in the previous two seasons and now Newcastle United were negotiating big money deals. Despite this, almost inexplicably, Sir Alex Ferguson sold three of his best players during the same summer and purchased no big signings as replacements. Paul Ince left to join Inter Milan for £7million, Andrei Kanchelskis was sold to Everton in a £5million deal and Mark Hughes moved to Chelsea for £1.5million. Manchester United's squad now seemed severely weakened by this and together with Eric Cantona serving a lengthy suspension and a squad littered with ageing players, United's chances of regaining the title seemed improbable.

On August 19th 1995 Manchester United fielded a team in their opening Premier League fixture against Aston Villa with an average age of under 24 years old. This was only increased by the ageing Peter Schmeichel, Paul Parker and Brian McClair who were all in their thirties. In the starting line-up Fergie included Phil and Gary Neville, Paul Scholes and Nicky Butt. John O'kane would replace Gary Pallister midway through the second half, however, on a legendary day in the history of Manchester United, it would be a second-half substitute that would make all the difference. After 45 minutes at Villa Park Manchester United were already 3-0 down against Aston Villa and during the break Alex Ferguson decided to bring on David Beckham. Manchester United ended up losing 3-1, yet their second half display inspired by a 19 year-old David Beckham proved to be a turning point in the eyes of the club. Beckham scored United's only goal and his first Premier League goal with a long range effort, which would not only prove to be a portent of his goal-scoring to come; it also showed that United's fledglings, albeit for only 45 minutes, could compete in the Premier League. Yet merely competing seemed a bizarre ambition for a man of Ferguson's stature. The United manager defiantly insisted that this team could win trophies, yet the media were having none of it. Match of the Day pundit Alan Hansen famously quoted "You can't win anything with kids." And everybody apart from those inside Old Trafford sided with the former Liverpool defender. This meant if Beckham and his young team mates were going to make it, they would have to become something special and pull off a feat that would emulate the revered uniqueness of the Busby Babes.

Despite the negativity surrounding the leap of faith the United manager had made when it came to his team selection, Ferguson stuck to his guns and continued to field a youthful side. United won their next two league games before travelling to reigning champions Blackburn Rovers at Ewood Park. The team that pipped United to the league title only three months earlier, would now face an allegedly weaker team after the big name departures from Old Trafford. However, it was David Beckham who curled in an instinctive winner with his back to goal in a 2-1 victory over the Champions. United's right-sided midfielder had now nailed his place in the side at the age of 19 along with the rest of the youth team graduates. Not only had they won three games on the bounce since the Villa Park set-back, they had now beaten the Premier League holders in their own back yard.

Beckham then scored in a 4-0 win over Coventry City before scoring a spectacular goal against Chelsea in October. However, the Reds went four games without a win, meaning Newcastle United now extended their lead at the top of the table to a seemingly unassailable twelve points. The promotion of Manchester United's class of '92 contingent to the first team seemed, at the least, too premature. Moreover, questions were emerging as to whether David Beckham and his fellow youth team graduates could emulate the great double winning team of 1994 in the coming years. Even if the 1995/1996 campaign was planned to be a season of transition, there was scarce evidence to suggest that success would come once the youngsters matured.

Then on New Year's Day 1996, Manchester United were crushed 4-1 away to Tottenham Hotspur. Kevin Pilkington, the goalkeeper who played with Beckham in the Youth Cup winning team replaced Peter Schmeichel in goal at half time. The Neville brothers who played in defence seemed to be losing the trust of the boss, as Sir Alex Ferguson threw in emergency loan signing William Prunier to bolster the defence. It turned out to be a catastrophic day for Fergie's young side. This result was seen to many as a day of reckoning. Alan Hansen's words at the beginning of the season were now revered as a wise portend. The kids had proved that they could compete at the top level, but trophies seemed far from imminent.

Alex Ferguson had emulated the great Sir Matt Busby by winning the league and even went one better by securing the club's first double. Yet the resurrection of Busby's youth philosophy seemed a nostalgic pseudo-reality which distorted the logic of how to achieve success in the modern era. The influx of expensive foreign stars and the increase in spending power had seen many clubs demanding instant glory. Manchester United appeared in danger of falling behind as a result of old-hand tactics. If Beckham and his fellow youngsters were not ready to deliver immediate success or prove they were capable of silverware in the future, then Fergie's summer overhaul would not look like the better side of judgement. The story of David

Beckham's rise from a Manchester United supporter who travelled north to achieve his dream had the foundations to be a fairy tale that could only be written at Old Trafford. However, reality had soon set in and the romantic story of Beckham and his fellow fledglings did not appear to be the fairy tale that was first proposed.

United's number 24 and the rest of the young players now needed to look for inspiration on and off the field. Auspiciously, it was Eric Cantona, United's current number seven who unknowingly became a role model for David Beckham and the rest of his teammates to aspire to. Eric Cantona was said to be Manchester United's most avid practiser and the Frenchman would often stay behind after training sessions to perfect his skills. When the rest of his teammates headed for the showers, Cantona would stay behind kicking balls into an empty net and rehearsing his unique tricks and flicks. David Beckham was the first to pick up on this, and proceeded to do the same by concentrating on extra training by repeatedly practising freekicks, corners and crosses. It was evident that Beckham admired Cantona from afar, he watched, he learned , he took note, and showed that he did not just want to a part of this team to play with a legendary number seven like Eric Cantona; he wanted to be a legendary number seven himself.

After the new year humiliation against Spurs, David Beckham only started in three of the next fifteen matches in all competitions. Although this would seem as a low point for the young United winger, one of the manager's traits was to not let any young player think that they have made the big time. Throughout his managing career, Sir Alex Ferguson was renowned for taking his young players in and out of the team to avoid any complacency or over-exposure.

During this period the Reds had managed to eke away at Newcastle United's 12 point lead. On February 25th 1996 Beckham started in a 6-0 victory over Bolton Wanderers where he scored his first headed goal for the club. United were now only four points behind Newcastle with a game in hand; and their next fixture was a trip to St James' Park to face the league leaders where a 1-0 victory brought United within touching distance to the top of the league.

As the season started to reach its climax, Manchester United now had an F.A. Cup semi-final to contend with and the Reds had to overcome Chelsea at Villa Park on March 31st 1996 in order to reach their third F.A. Cup final in a row. United found themselves 1-0 down at half-time; and the question marks still remained as to whether Ferguson's injection of youth could take United to cup finals in the consistent fashion of his previous teams. The Reds equalised just after half-time through Andy Cole and moments later a misplaced back pass from Chelsea defender Craig Burley saw Beckham through on goal.

It is these moments that can define a player, they can make-or-break a career, they separate the good from the great, the achievers from the underachievers. When a young player who's place in the team is in doubt sees the whites of the goalkeepers eyes in a semi-final match with a chance to put his team into a final, many would crumble under the pressure. However, in that heart skipping moment, Beckham coolly slotted the ball past Chelsea's Kevin Hitchcock to make the score 2-1 to the Reds which booked their place at Wembley.

On May 11th 1996 David Beckham was making his first F.A. Cup final appearance for the Reds, however, the United number 24 proved he was no shrinking violet. With five minutes to go and the score locked at 0-0, United won a corner right in front of their own fans, with the spectators roaring at the young right-winger with hair-raising enthusiasm. As Beckham swung the ball in from the right, a melee occurred in the box resulting in Cantona scoring the winner. A Beckham corner which the opposition had failed to defend had now produced an iconic moment for United's current number seven Eric Cantona; and with his whole career ahead of him, it was evident that more iconic moments were set to be created from his set pieces. Moreover, he looked to have the potential to one day produce his own magic wearing the coveted number seven shirt himself.

Beckham started the 1996/1997 campaign wearing the vacant number ten shirt left by Mark Hughes and proceeded to play the same way he ended the previous season, by scoring a spectacular goal against Newcastle United in the Charity Shield at Wembley. Yet it was his next match which redefined the semantics and boundaries of the word spectacular forever.

On August 17th 1996 Manchester United travelled to Selhurst Park to play Wimbledon for their first Premier League fixture of the

1996/1997 season. The Reds were soon 2-0 up thanks to goals from Denis Irwin and Eric Cantona. As the game wore on, United's then number seven Cantona was substituted late on and watched the remaining minutes from the touch line. As the ball broke to Brian McClair he fed a pass to Beckham who found himself a few yards of space in his own half, before glancing goalwards. David Beckham had previously attempted similar attempts in the match, and Sir Alex Ferguson famously said to his assistant that any further attempts would lead to his substitution. Nevertheless, without taking a touch he then struck the ball on the halfway line, which then sailed over the stranded 'Dons goalkeeper Neil Sullivan and in to the middle of the net.

George Best had previously tried such an audacious attempt for Manchester United which came close, then in 1993 Eric Cantona hit the cross bar with a similar long range effort against Chelsea. Even the great Pele failed with an attempt from inside his own half. However, if emulation was part of Beckham's desire to be great, it was the outdoing of two of the previous number sevens that must have become even higher on his agenda.

Between Beckham replacing number seven Andrei Kanchelskis in 1992 to the current number seven watching from the bench, the United midfielder appeared to have conjured-up a one man mission to prove he was worthy of one day wearing the famous shirt. His all-time hero was Bryan Robson, his current role-model was Eric Cantona. To claim the the coveted shroud it seemed he would have to do something extraordinary to earn its ownership; and on the August 17th 1996, the young lad from North London scored a far from ordinary goal, to place himself as heir to a far from ordinary shirt.

His next goal came against Derby County three games later which, in any other season could have been a 'goal of the season' contender as he astonishingly smashed the ball into the top corner from twenty five yards. He then scored two Champions League goals either side of another long-range goal, this time it was a winner against Liverpool in the Premier League after driving the ball home from outside the box.

After an unbeaten nine game start to the 1996/1997 season, United then hit a low point. First they were beaten 5-0 by Newcastle United, which was there biggest Premier League defeat to date, then they suffered a 6-3 defeat to Southampton at The Dell on the October 26th 1996. Beckham did, however, score his first free-kick for the Reds in this match. The Saints even had a defender on the line as extra protection; yet United's number ten confidently curled the ball home from outside the box, in the same corner as the covering defender. The Reds then lost their unbeaten home European record to the unfancied Turkish outfit Fenerbahce in a 1-0 defeat, before suffering their third league loss in a row with Chelsea winning 2-1 at Old Trafford, which was their first top-flight defeat at home since December 1994.

Manchester United responded by going sixteen league games unbeaten and it was in this time that Beckham started adding to his portfolio of spectacular goals. The 22-year-old was now becoming England's most exciting player with the ball at his feet when standing outside the box. After two sublime chipped goals against West Ham and Nottingham Forest in December, he then scored another free kick against Tottenham in the F.A.Cup 3rd round in January. He then caused Spurs more heartbreak in their next league match on January 12th 1997 when he took the ball midway through his opponents half, before striking a long-range effort from nearly 30 yards which bent away from Spurs goalkeeper Ian Walker and into the top right corner of the net. This goal not only earned United a dramatic late win at White Hart Lane, it also proved that Beckham was now approaching the world class bracket as a player. Moreover, he was single-handedly drawing up the short list for the goal of the season.

As the season entered the final stages, Beckham added one more goal to his collection. This time a crashing volley against Chelsea in a 1-1 draw. United's attention soon shifted to the Champions League and in particular David Beckham, as an injury depleted midfield saw United's number ten line up alongside centre-half Ronny Johnsen in the heart of their midfield. Beckham, who had played most of his early career on the right wing, was now playing a more central role in the biggest game at Old Trafford for years. Fergie's men romped away to a 4-0 victory over a Porto side that had won all of their group matches and were favourites to lift the trophy at the time. Beckham proved that night that he was not just a one-trick pony. His energy in midfield together with radar-like passes and dribbling skills proved he was becoming the complete player. After performing so competently in such a high profile Champions League game despite being out of position, Alex Ferguson knew he had the option to do so again. Perhaps this match was on omen, as history would go on to tell us.

United eventually lost in the semi-final of the Champions League that year. Despite dominating both legs against Borussia Dortmund, the Reds were eliminated 2-0 on aggregate. Some saw this as progress for United's young blossoming side despite the disappointment. Nonetheless, United did go on to win the league, which was all but sealed in a 3-1 win against Liverpool, where two Beckham corners provided the assists for United's first two goals, which were nodded in by Gary Pallister, before a third by Andy Cole. It was not until the penultimate game of the season that United were confirmed Champions, yet it was clear that this team was not a flash in the pan, and further glory seemed imminent for Beckham and company, both at home and abroad. Furthermore, David Beckham won The PFA Young Player of the Year Award for his spectacular scrap book of goals and his all-round playing ability. He had also established himself as a regular in the England squad during the 1996/1997 season and everything pointed towards a career of superstardom for the player, who two years ago was playing lower league football.

From the Back page to the front

The 1997/1998 season was a big season for David Beckham as England were heading towards their first world cup since 1990. Having won the PFA Young Player of the Year in the previous season he now had to live up to the hype that was surrounding his football. Yet it was this campaign where the hype off the football field started to grow around David Beckham and juggling the two burdens for the biggest club in the world could have the potential to turn into a disaster for any footballer.

On May 18th 1997, Eric Cantona retired as a player and left the coveted number seven shirt free to claim. With Teddy Sheringham arriving from Tottenham Hotspur, potentially as Cantona's short-term successor, Beckham left his number ten shirt for Sheringham and picked up the iconic number seven jersey for himself.

The time had come for Beckham to wear the empowering garment that was donned by his childhood hero Bryan Robson. He appeared ready as a player, however, if the media hysteria that suffocated George Best and Eric Cantona was to hang around his neck like a sodden fleece, the question remained as to whether he would be ready to carry that off too.

David Beckham's first three Premier League appearances of the 1997/1998 season came as a substitute, and in the second match of this sequence he scored his first goal as United's number seven. With United struggling to open the deadlock in a dull game against Southampton, it was Beckham who fired the late winner, just like his number seven predecessor Cantona did on so many occasions when his team needed him the most. The young Englishman then netted against Everton two games later in a 2-0 win at Goodison Park, with United's new number ten Teddy Sheringham bagging the second goal.

The reigning Young Player of the Year was in the spotlight as far as the impending World Cup was concerned, however, the spotlight that could shine from the media was also about to be turned on. Unbeknown to Beckham, his private life was about to become a tabloid dream for the predators that lay in wait. On November 1st 1997 David Beckham met Victoria Adams, a member of the British pop group the Spice Girls, in the player's lounge after beating Sheffield Wednesday 6-1 at Old Trafford. This encounter would lead to them starting a relationship.

If the great Cantona intended to use his famous words about the media as a non-sequitur, then perhaps the analogy was more suited to this case, as the seagulls of the national press circled, waiting for a net-full of rumours to be unleashed into the sea of showbiz. Yet United's number seven continued to do his talking on the pitch and on November 22nd 1997 he came on as a substitute against Wimbledon and scored 40 seconds after entering the field. Beckham then scored a long range deflected second in a resounding 5-2 score line at Selhurst Park. When United travelled to Anfield on December 6th 1997 they were riding high at the top of the league and had netted 24 goals in their previous five matches. It was Beckham's precocious right boot that scored United's second goal in a 3-1 score line, this time from a free-kick, which flew in off the underside of the bar.

At the turn of the year, away from football David Beckham announced his engagement to girlfriend Victoria, but on the field his attention, and everyone else's in England, turned to the World Cup in the summer of 1998. Many of United's English stars were looking to impress manager Glenn Hoddle to earn their selection and it was felt that United's class of '92 contingent were going to be a major part of his squad. Beckham made a statement of intent in the F.A. Cup third round on January 4th 1998 when he scored two goals in a 5-3 win over Chelsea at Stamford Bridge. United's overall form then dipped over the coming weeks, with shock defeats to Coventry, Southampton and Leicester severely hampering their title charge. Beckham did score another trademark goal against Aston Villa early in February, in a 2-0 win which saw Beckham jumping into the delirious United fans at Villa Park. Nonetheless, this delirium was short lived, as the coming month saw United's elimination from the F.A. Cup after losing to an unfancied Barnsley team, then a Champions League exit to Monaco in the quarter-finals of the Champions League.

Despite having a twelve point advantage over Arsenal in the league earlier in the year, Arsenal then defeated United at Old Trafford in what proved to be a title decider. Marc Overmars hit a late winner for the Gunners who then won their remaining games of the season, before clinching the Premier League title. United did go unbeaten for the rest of the season after this defeat with Beckham adding three more goals to take his season's tally to eleven, yet it became a year to forget for Sir Alex Ferguson's men. David Beckham and his teammates, who started the campaign so strongly in all competitions, had aspirations of a spectacular season, yet they capitulated in the final fixtures. With United no longer hampered by the foreigner rule in Europe and boasting a large squad of players, they saw the 1997/1998 campaign, which was exactly forty years after the Munich Air Disaster and thirty years after they last won the European Cup, as the season that would finally end their Champions League woes. It was not to be, and David Beckham turned his attention to what seemed to be a timely distraction, the 1998 World Cup in France.

Beckham did not start in England's first two group games against Tunisia and Romania, however, his first start of the tournament against Columbia saw United's number seven score a trademark free kick. England's qualification meant that they would now face Argentina in the last sixteen of the knock-out stages. Early in the second half of this match with the game locked at 2-2, David Beckham, who was lay on the floor, aimed a flicked heel towards Diego Simeone. The Argentina captain then fell to the ground which prompted the referee to show the United midfielder a red card.

The height of David Beckham's profile became evident on many counts that day. If United's number seven was not perceived as having superstar status before this match, then the whole world knew about him now. His ascent to fame had already been complete and it was this incident that proved the magnitude of his stardom. Although kicking out at an opponent will always run the risk of being sent off, the questions remained as to whether the Argentinian players set out to ruffle his feathers, a tactic only deployed on the most dangerous of players. Perhaps the occasion and the name of the player forced the referee into a hasty decision. Nevertheless, it rocked the world of football; and if the events on the field that day caused shockwaves, the events that unfolded afterwards escalated into a full scale earthquake.

England eventually lost 4-3 in a penalty shoot-out, however, the players that missed that day, Paul Ince and David Batty were never even slightly cajoled, unlike previous tournaments where Chris Waddle's and Gareth Southgate's penalty misses in 1990 and 1996 respectively made them the nations burden bearers. This time it appeared to be all Beckham's fault; and the country was not going to allow him to forget it.

There comes a time in every number seven's life at Manchester United where they build up to a climax of footballing genius, before crashing down to the lowest parameter of sporting life. Best, Robson and Cantona has risen in a Lazarus like fashion from this void, but it was hard to decipher whether a young David Beckham, who had his whole life documented on the front pages of the national newspapers, would be able to return from the football oblivion that the number sevens of Manchester United are perpetually cast into.

The Treble

David Beckham was now public enemy number one in England. His blossoming career had hit a brick wall, as the nation and the press had a field day that summer. There was speculation of a move abroad for Beckham, who was about to face the impending backlash from rival supporters who held him personally accountable for England's loss.

Beckham made the decision to stay at Old Trafford knowing he had the backing of the club and his teammates. Manchester United and Alex Ferguson stood by their troubled number seven, just like they did with Eric Cantona three years earlier. The Reds were firmly in the 'them against us' mind-set at the start of the 1998-1999 season, which could see United crumbling under a siege mentality from the press, opposing fans and opposing football clubs. On-the-other-hand, it could galvanise a team spirit, which is drawn from the life-blood of Manchester United's philosophy of never-say-die and thriving in the face of adversity.

As they entered the final campaign of the twentieth century, United had the chance to prove that the century belonged to them, and to do so Manchester United and David Beckham would have to pull-off a remarkable feat in order to make this happen.

The Reds had splashed out on Jaap Stam, Dwight Yorke and Jesper Blomqvist that summer in an attempt to re-establish themselves as the top dogs in England once more, after Arsenal had won the double in the previous season. United's journey as challengers started off badly as they suffered a 3-0 defeat to Arsenal at Wembley in the Charity Shield. Fergie's men then then played their first Premier League game of the season against Leicester City at Old Trafford on the August 15th 1998, where David Beckham felt the wrath of the away fans throughout the game, as they booed United's number seven every time he touched the ball. This appeared to affect United's performance and they saw themselves 2-0 down with ten minutes to go. The Reds pulled one back with time running out after Beckham saw his shot on goal diverted into the net by Teddy Sheringham, then in the fourth minute of stoppage time United were awarded a free-kick outside the box. Beckham, who had suffered throughout the whole match, stood behind the ball knowing that if an attempt on goal drifted wide of the target then United would lose the match. This was a test of character for the young winger, as his sky-high confidence which saw him scoring from any distance in the previous four seasons had not been evident as of yet. The Leicester City defence even organised themselves in order to defend a cross rather than a shot. Nonetheless, Beckham bent the ball home from thirty yards, sending Old Trafford into raptures and proving that the events of the summer had not affected him.

United's next encounter came against West Ham United at Upton Park, who's ardent England contingent made an effigy of David Beckham in a noose outside the ground, before a 0-0 draw was played out. It was evident that this season would not see United's number seven merely being the pantomime villain. He was now public enemy number one in England, however, he did gain some sanctuary in the Reds' European games. United's first group game in the Champions League that year saw Beckham curl in another one of his trademark free-kicks against the mighty Barcelona. His icy glare and ankle-breaking technique culminated in the ball bulging the top corner of the net in a pulsating 3-3 draw at Old Trafford.

United suffered a sketchy start to the 1998/1999 season domestically after losing to reigning champions Arsenal again in the league and notching up too many draws. Despite this, the goals were still flowing for United after Andy Cole and Dwight Yorke formed a lethal partnership in front of goal; and it was United's number seven, David Beckham who was providing most of the assists.
Beckham scored another long-ranger in a 5-1 win over Wimbledon in the league at Old Trafford, before arcing in another free kick two weeks later in a 5-0 win over Brondby in the Champions League. Soon United were scoring goals for fun and playing the most exciting football that any team had produced in years, yet their gung-ho approach caused them to leak goals at the other end and the results were becoming too inconsistent.

One of the finest games in United's history occurred on the 25th November 1998 when the Reds fought-out another ding-dong 3-3 draw against Barcelona in the Champions League, this time at the Nou Camp. It was Yorke and Cole who provided the goals, and Beckham provided the assist for the third goal when he crossed the ball for

Yorke to head home. United were playing with no fear and were embracing an all-out attack mentality against the biggest teams in Europe, with Beckham's crosses mesmerising the defenders on the continent who rarely had to deal with such a weapon in their respective domestic leagues.

December became a difficult month for United during this season. After being eliminated by Tottenham Hotspur in the League Cup, they went five matches without a win. Amidst this run, Beckham faced more abuse when United drew 2-2 with Spurs in the league, however, the United winger provided both assists from crosses, which resulted in Ole Gunnar Solskjaer netting twice. Another draw against Bayern Munich at Old Trafford saw United progress to the quarter-finals of the Champions League, yet on December 19th 1998 the Reds suffered their first home defeat of the season in a 3-2 loss to Middlesbrough.

United entered the new year in bad shape, with three losses already in the league, only two wins out of six in the Champions League group stages and elimination from the League Cup. The systematic jeers and heckling from rival supporters towards Beckham did not seem to rattle him, although United's inconsistency was proving to be a stumbling block for any aspirations to succeed in 1999.

Sometimes in football, a culmination of factors, influences and catalysts can dictate how a season unfolds. United's success to this point in the nineties had never been plain sailing. They had the ability to win by big score-lines, however, they quite often had to grind out results or work themselves out of difficult situations. The turn of the year saw them thrash West Ham 4-1 at Old Trafford and then Leicester 6-2 at Filbert Street, in a game where Beckham provided the assist for Jaap Stam's only goal of his United career.

Then on January 24th 1999 Manchester United played Liverpool in the F.A. Cup 4th round. What occurred that day was a spine-chilling portent, which kick-started United to go on a run in the league and cup competitions. This run dared Manchester United to believe in something that they were told could never be achieved in football. It was around this time that Sir Alex Ferguson called his team's quest for the treble 'The Impossible Dream'. With two minutes to go in the tie at Old Trafford, the Reds were 1-0 behind after a Michael Owen goal early in the first half. United were heading out of the Cup until Beckham stood behind another free kick outside the box, which at first appeared to be in shooting range for someone of his calibre. This time Beckham did not go for goal, instead the United number seven floated in a pinpoint cross where Dwight Yorke equalised after an Andy Cole knock-down. It looked all set for the daunting prospect of a replay at Anfield, until Solskjaer found himself with the ball inside the box during stoppage time. As Solskjaer netted the winner in a comeback which all started at the feet of David Beckham, United fans were sent into ecstasy as the game finished 2-1.

Something big happened that day and the effervescent glow of footballing magic seemed to rub off on United's upcoming fixtures.

Ever since the Munich Air Disater in 1958, Manchester United have embraced a rich philosophy based on youth which stemmed from the Busby Babes and the resilience to never accept defeat, after the club rebuilt itself to return back to the promised land after that fateful day. This is where the soul of the club became established and the mantra of never giving up became instilled in that team from that day forward.

The residual aftershock of the game against Liverpool overlapped into the next set of fixtures; and David Beckham became an integral part of the final stretch of the season. On February 6th 1999 - the 41st anniversary of the Munich Air Distaster, Manchester United hammered Nottingham Forest 8-1 at the City Ground, with David Beckham having a hand in creating six of the goals from the right side of midfield. After progressing to the quarter-finals of the F.A. Cup at the expense of Fulham, United then won their next two games with Beckham's crosses creating the winners in a 1-0 win at Coventry and a 2-1 victory over Southampton. United's number seven then unleashed his most potent weapon on Europe's elite, with Beckham providing two untameable crosses against Inter Milan in the quarter-finals of the Champions League, where Dwight Yorke converted both goals in a 2-0 win at Old Trafford. United then progressed to the semi-finals of the Champions League after a 1-1 draw in the second leg in Italy. In between these matches the Reds also secured qualification to the last four of the F.A. Cup with a 2-0 replay win over Chelsea. United's next league game saw Beckham curl in another trademark free-kick against Everton in a 3-1 win on March 21st 1999, before netting the equaliser in a 1-1 draw against Wimbledon. Beckham was coming into his own in the home straight of the 1998/1999 season, with the midfielder both scoring and creating goals. Now, the stakes were getting higher and Manchester United were heading deep into uncharted territory.

On the April 7th 1999 the Reds now faced the tournament favourites Juventus in the last four of the Champions League, a team who had appeared in the previous three finals. It seemed a daunting prospect for Fergie's men against the likes of Zidane, Davids and Deschamps and the first leg of this semi-final encounter at Old Trafford saw United fall behind early in the match with a goal from Antonio Conte. Yet United's resilience, that had gathered momentum in recent months saw them eventually equalise in injury time after David Beckham's looping, hopeful cross ended in Ryan Giggs snatching a lifeline to take to Turin.

United's next match came four days later in the F.A. Cup semi-final against Arsenal at Villa Park. The game finished 0-0, so in the replay on April 14th 1999 Sir Alex Ferguson rung the changes to the dismay of many, as Cole and Yorke were left out of the starting line-up and Ryan Giggs was on the bench. However, despite their absences, the game itself had everything. United took the lead with a Beckham special after Sheringham had laid the ball off to the United number seven outside the Arsenal penalty area. Beckham then curled the ball first time from twenty five yards past the outstretched arm of David Seaman and into the Arsenal net. United looked in control for most of the game until midway through the second half their quest for the treble looked like imploding. First Arsenal equalised through a deflected Bergkamp effort and then the Gunners had a goal disallowed for offside which took them 30 seconds to realise. Roy Keane was then sent off for a second bookable offence and as United tried to hold on, they conceded a penalty in the last minute of the game. However, Peter Schmeichel in his last season for United heroically saved Bergkamp's spot-kick. David Beckham rushed to hug the Great Dane, yet the United goalkeeper pushed any celebrations away and the Reds lived on into extra-time. With Arsenal having the advantage of an extra man, Beckham and his teammates were hanging on for their F.A.

Cup lives against the reigning double holders and Schmeichel had to be repeatedly called into action. Soon United were holding on for a penalty shoot-out but a sloppy pass by Vieira gave the ball to Ryan Giggs in his own half. With running- down the clock being the order of the day, the Welsh wizard looked ahead at what was in front of him. It was the best defence in Europe who just did not concede goals. They were the gate-keepers to United's chance of a treble and the best hope that Ryan Giggs had was to run the ball down to the corner flag.

If there is one thing that is encouraged as a Manchester United youngster, it is going on the field and expressing yourself. United's class of '92 embraced this and continued to do what they did on the patches of grass in Salford as kids all the way through their careers. If Beckham's style of play had been restricted, then he would not have attempted to shoot from distance, which gave United the lead earlier in the game. If his F.A. Youth Cup winning teammate Ryan Giggs had been restricted in his career, he would, and probably should have ran down the clock, considering that they had a man sent-off and were playing against the Premier League and F.A. Cup holders.

Giggsy had a different plan though, a plan so unbelievable that it would bring football history to its knees. On a 60 yard run, he turned each member of Arsenals back four inside out, then smashed the ball past the England number one David Seaman to give United the most unlikeliest of leads. The Reds hung on and soon the impossible dream became more probable for Sir Alex Ferguson.

The celebrations that unfolded were some of the most amazing scenes ever seen in F.A. Cup history. Manchester United fans flooded onto the pitch and carried David Beckham and Ryan Giggs off the field on their shoulders. United's number seven was now a football God to them and he was being worshipped in the same way Cantona was lauded in 1996 when he returned from his ban to help United's kids win the double and in the same way Bryan Robson was carried of the pitch against Barcelona in 1984.

There was barely time for the euphoria to die down when David Beckham and his Manchester United teammates travelled to Turin to face Juventus in the second leg of the Champions League semi-final on April 21st 1999. United were 2-0 down to the home side after 11 minutes, and after scraping a 1-1 draw in the first leg of this semi-final at Old Trafford, United found themselves with the task of overturning a 3-1 deficit at the Stadio Delle Alpi. A David Beckham set-piece then helped to produce another iconic moment in the clubs history as his corner saw United captain Roy Keane pull one back for the Reds with a header midway through the first half to give United hope. Moments later the Irishman was booked for a foul on Zinedine Zidane which meant that Keane would miss the Champions League final. Roy Keane then re-wrote the manual on influential midfield play as the game finished 3-2 with further goals from Yorke and Cole, meaning the Reds progressed to the final 4-3 on aggregate. However a Paul Scholes yellow card in the second half meant that another central midfielder would also miss the final. United were going to Barcelona, but sadly for Keane and Scholes they were not. As the celebrations subsided, it was evident that there was only one recognised central midfielder available for selection in Nicky Butt.

United's attention turned back to the Premier League and on May 1st 1999 they went one step closer to reclaiming the title with a 2-1 victory over Aston Villa. It was David Beckham who scored the winner with one of his finest ever free kicks, by whipping the ball into the top corner from thirty yards. Four days later United then drew 2-2 with Liverpool at Anfield, with Beckham's pin-point cross allowing Dwight Yorke to open the scoring with a far-post header. A Denis Irwin penalty put United 2-0 in front, however, a string of calamitous decisions by referee David Ellary allowed Liverpool to comeback. A 1-0 win over Middlesbrough preceded a 0-0 draw against Blackburn Rovers, which meant that United had to win their final game of the season against Tottenham Hotspur to become champions once more. Not for the first time this season, United made it hard for themselves after Les Ferdinand put the visitors ahead early in the first half. United then failed to convert a string of chances, before David Beckham equalised with a curling effort from just inside the box. Just like in the F.A. Cup semi-final against Arsenal, David Beckham was producing his best moments in the biggest games, as he opened the scoring by manipulating the ball with his unique curl and trajectory; the very technique that was regimented into his golden right boot after years of incessant training and practise. After Andy Cole scored the winner early in the second half United were crowned Premier League champions for the fifth time in seven seasons.

Six days later United won the F.A Cup at Wembley, with Sheringham and Scholes scoring the vital goals, securing their third double in six seasons. Now Beckham and his teammates were heading into the biggest match of their lives, however, where Sir Alex Ferguson could afford to rest some of his stars against Newcastle in the F.A. Cup Final, the United manager now had a selection problem on his hands, due to the suspensions of Keane and Scholes. Many assumed the versatile Ronny Johnsen would move up into midfield. Others suggested playing three up front which worked in the previous match at Wembley, as Sheringham came on early to replace the injured Roy Keane. Yet as the team news was announced, it revealed that Beckham would partner Nicky Butt in the centre of midfield, with Jesper Blomqvist and Ryan Giggs starting on the wings.

On May 26th 1999, in the biggest game of all, United had gone behind early in the game to a Mario Basler free-kick. This was a team so efficiently German that an equaliser seemed the most unlikeliest of scenarios in the Champions League Final at the Nou Camp. The Bayern Munich defenders knew who they marking, when they were marking them and how they should be marked. United were unlucky not to have fallen further behind after Bayern rattled the United woodwork twice. This was the situation until Peter Schmeichel pottered forward into the opposing box with time running out after United won a corner, which Beckham would take. For the first time in the game the German champions did not know who to mark and as the ball was cleared, the Bayern defenders were drawn to Schmeichel's green jersey like flies to a blue lamp. This confusion allowed substitute Teddy Sheringham to convert a sequence of miss-kicks into the Bayern goal 30 seconds into stoppage time after United trailed 1-0 since the 6th minute. The late leveller looked to have dramatically forced the game into extra-time, but this was Matt Busby's 90th birthday, this was against a team from Munich, so fortunately the footballing Gods had other ideas. In the third minute of stoppage time, another corner from David Beckham was flicked on by Sheringham and in the greatest comeback of all 'Solskjaer had won it'. The impossible dream had become a reality.

David Beckham's corners that led to the United goals created the most unimaginable fairy tale in football. Yet his influence on the team in the years preceding this match meant that it was no surprise that Beckham was the creator of these moments. A player who was often forced into the limelight by the media off the field would paradoxically create the limelight for his teammates on the field. From his corner that led to Cantona scoring in the F.A Cup final in 1996, to his freekick in the F.A. Cup 4th Round in 1999 which led to United's equaliser against Liverpool in another astonishing comeback, Beckham became the pen that wrote the scripts for the other players to be the stars of the show. His goal in the F.A. Cup semi-final replay against Arsenal in 1999 meant that the game went to extra-time which led to Ryan Giggs scoring the greatest F.A. Cup goal of all time. His corner which was headed in by Roy Keane in the semi-final of the Champions league against Juventus a week later was the catalyst for the United captain to put in one of the best individual displays on a football pitch ever seen, despite Keane being banned for the final.

His unavoidable ascent into the celebrity world outside of football did not hamper his role at United during the treble season. Beckham made 23 assists in all competitions, and this incredible tally of creativity confounds the fact that David Beckham the footballer was the man behind the scenes. He was writing the plot for other players to become the famous characters in a season that even Hollywood could not script. However, only time would tell if the media frenzy surrounding Beckham would put him into the limelight too much and force him out into his own individual stardom, rather than being a vital cog that was part of United's treble winning wheel.

Beckham was now fast becoming an global icon and his interest in fashion and his popstar girlfriend was giving opposition fans more excuses to dislike United. There was still resentment from his red card in the World Cup during the summer of 1998 and his appearances for England were being greeted by boos from the England fans.

The abuse that Beckham was receiving became intolerable during a 3–2 loss to Portugal in Euro 2000. Despite Beckham creating two goals, many England supporters still taunted him throughout the game. Beckham then aimed a middle finger gesture at his detractors, which was met by criticism from the press, however, some of the media that had indulged in previous animosity towards the United star had now hypocritically suggested that the abuse should stop. Then on November 15th 2000, the United number seven was given the captain's armband by the England caretaker manager Peter Taylor and then continued as skipper under the new boss Sven-Göran Eriksson.

As for club football, he was still idolised by the United fans and if anything, the coldness from the English press and English football fans made the Old Trafford faithful warm to their number seven even more. David Beckham was still only 23 years old and like many of his other class of '92 teammates, he was still years away from his peak. Yet they had already reached the pinnacle of their careers in terms of domestic and European achievement, after becoming the first English team to win the Treble. The hunger and never-say-die attitude that epitomised their unrivalled success in 1999 was going to be difficult to continue throughout the rest of their time at the club. It also seemed that if the treble was to be achieved again by an English team, it could never be done again in such a dramatic fashion.

The 1999/2000 season started with a 2-1 defeat to Arsenal in the Charity Shield, however, United's League form continued to be impressive as they remained unbeaten until the start of October, with Beckham playing in all but one of those games. Yet in the midst of this good run of league form, the Reds lost the European Super Cup Final to Lazio and their Champions League form was indifferent after the holders lost away to Marseille in the group stages. Beckham's first goal of the season came against Croatia Zagreb when he netted another trademark free-kick in a 2-1 win. Then on November 30th 1999 he started in United's 1-0 triumph over Palmeiras in the Intercontinental Cup. Beckham then played in his and arguably United's best game of the season when they beat Valencia 3-0 at Old Trafford, with Beckham setting up two of United's goals with a dazzling display on the right side of midfield.

If the previous season was one of the most dramatic ever seen, then the 1999/2000 season was perhaps the most controversial. After winning the Champions League the year before, United were then invited to take part in part in the World Club Championships in Brazil. This tournament meant that three matches would be played at the Maracana in a group style format. The Reds' were encouraged not to take part in the F.A. Cup by the F.A. as they wanted an English representative abroad and the fixtures that they would miss at home would be logistically impossible to rearrange. David Beckham's last venture onto the World stage saw him sent off for England; and when United kicked off their first game against Rayos Del Necaxa on January 6th 2000, history would repeat itself.

United went one-nil down to the Mexican side before Beckham was sent-off at the end of the first half for a high-booted challenge on Jose Milian. United battled back to earn a point with Bosnich even saving a penalty for the Reds in a controversial match. The red card for Beckham seemed harsh, however, the incessant jeers from the crowd seemed to have rattled the United number seven reviving doubts over his unpredictable temperament, particularly on the world stage. United ended up leaving the tournament early after failing to qualify from their group, with Beckham missing the 3-1 defeat against Vasco de Game through suspension and failing to make the starting line-up against Melbourne. Yet it was David Beckham who would steal the headlines again. Since the sending off against Argentina in the World Cup the abuse David Beckham received from opposing fans and the press was vitriolic. Now the media had another stick to beat Beckham with after he received his marching orders in Brazil.

United returned home still having the Premier League and Champions League to concentrate on, yet despite the team's month away from domestic action, they came back to England still near the top of the league and had several games in hand over their rivals, who failed to capitalise in the absence of Fergie's men. In the first match back on home soil on January 24th 2000 David Beckham set up a Sheringham equaliser in a 1-1 draw with Arsenal, before scoring a last gasp winner himself against Middlesbrough at Old Trafford in a 1-0 win four days later. It was evident that the red card in Brazil had somehow inspired him to produce his best form again for the club, just as he did after the sending-off for England in 1998.

On March 18th 2000 United's number seven scored a free-kick against Leicester City in a 2-0 win. The headlines the next day should have been about how the United winger curled another dead ball into the opposition net, however, it was his new haircut that grabbed the headlines. His floppy blonde locks had now gone and he was instead sporting a shaven head. Perhaps this was an act of rebellion to rid himself of the portrayed image that the media and opposition fans unjustifiably had of him. Either way, it was an example of how Beckham the footballer and Beckham the celebrity were no longer separate entities. None-the-less, just as his haircut made the front page, it did not take away his image of a footballer to his adoring fans. Those that wore the number seven shirt and had a Beckham hair cut now had shaved heads just like their idol. Yet this was not media hype influencing the United fans, this was the purely the magic of the number seven shirt. This was no different to the fans of George Best having rock and roll haircuts, or the way that Eric Cantona's following popped their collars and stuck out their chests.

By the start of March, United were seven points clear at the top of the league and had secured qualification to the quarter finals of the Champions League, which would be a two-legged tie against Real Madrid. It was on March 25th 2000 that Beckham saved his best corner since the Champions League final in 1999, when he floated the ball to the edge of the box for Paul Scholes to hit first time on the volley. Beckham himself had already scored that day, before Scholes had netted the goal of the season in a 4-0 win over Bradford City at Valley Parade. Then in United's next match, Beckham set up two goals and scored another eye-defying free-kick against West Ham in 7-1 thrashing at Old Trafford. The Reds were in rampant form in the Premier League; and now their attentions turned to the Champions League, where they looked to retain the trophy that they had dramatically won the year before.

The First leg of the last-eight match-up with Real Madrid saw United claim a decent 0-0 draw in the Bernabeu. Yet this meant that Fergie's men had to win at Old Trafford in order to progress to the semi-finals once more. The return leg two weeks later began disastrously for United as they found themselves 3-0 down early in the second half. Beckham then pulled one goal back with a superb solo goal after jinking past two defenders, before unleashing a powerful shot into the top corner of the net. Paul Scholes then added a second, yet despite the late rally United lost 3-2 and were eliminated from the Champions League.

Their next match was against Southampton where United clinched the Premier League title with a 3-1 victory at the Dell. Beckham added to his season's tally with another perfectly executed free-kick which crashed into the top corner despite the Saint's having defenders on the line as cover. The celebrations after the game were somewhat anti-climactic given their exit from Europe three days before. The Reds did finish their domestic campaign in style by winning their last eleven league games in a row, with Beckham adding another screamer to his repertoire on the final home game of the season in a 3-1 win over Spurs. This run of games saw the Reds win the league by an eighteen point margin, yet their failure to reach the heights of the previous season combined with the disappointment in the World Club Championships, meant it was a bitter sweet season for Sir Alex Ferguson's boys, and another controversial chapter in the career of David Beckham.

The 2000-2001 season started well for David Beckham, as he scored four goals in the opening seven matches. He was not only finding the net on a regular basis this season, he was also terrorising defenders with his crosses from the right of midfield. By the time the Red's had to face the newly promoted Manchester City for the first time since 1996, on November 18th 2000, Beckham had already created twelve goals.

David Beckham did not take long in stamping his authority on the game when United were awarded a free-kick 25 yards from goal in the first minute of the match. The United number seven then bent in arguably one of his greatest free-kicks past the outstretched Nicky Weaver into the City net. Delirious celebrations ensued after the goal, which eventually turned out to be the winner. Beckham then ended the year by setting up Solskjaer to score a late winner against Aston Villa on Boxing Day, followed by a goal from the penalty spot against Newcastle four days later.

United's re-entry into the F.A. Cup was short lived after they were knocked out in the fourth round against West Ham on January 28th 2001. However, they were firmly in the driving seat once more in the league. An unbeaten run in all competitions up until a 2-0 defeat against Liverpool in March saw United progress to the quarter-finals of the Champions League once more and notch up an unassailable lead at the top of the Premier League. United's European venture was cut short in the last eight by Bayern Munich. In their first meeting since United won the final in 1999, Bayern beat Beckham and company 3-1 on aggregate to knock the Reds out of Europe. United did, however, achieve their third Premier League crown in a row in their second league game after this defeat. Beckham was once again the provider as he set up the goal of the game which was scored by Paul Scholes in a 4-2 win. The joy of victory was once more mixed with deflation after the recent European elimination, yet Beckham had been a part of Manchester United making history, as the club won the top-flight division in three consecutive seasons for the very first time. In the summer before the 2001/2002 season Sir Alex Ferguson splashed out on record transfer deals to bring Ruud Van Nistelrooy and Juan Sebastien Veron to the club. Fergie wanted to rule Europe once more and felt that parts of the treble winning squad were coming to the end of their peak. Beckham, however, was in the prime of his life; and a big year was in stall for the United number seven, both for club and for country.

Beckham started the 2001/2002 season in prolific fashion, scoring a free-kick on the opening day of the season against Fulham in a 3-2 win, before netting a late equaliser during a 2-2 draw in United's next match, with a delightful chip against Blackburn Rovers at Ewood Park. After scoring against Everton in a 4-1 win early in September, Beckham was then the saviour in United's first Champion's League match ten days later against Lille Metropole, where he scored an injury time winner in a 1-0 win. His explosive start to this season continued when the Reds went to White Hart Lane on September 29th 2001. Despite Beckham's goal scoring form, United had been week defensively so far this season and leading up to this match United had recently lost 4-3 away to Newcastle United and then 2-1 to Deportivo La Coruna in Spain.

By half time in this match against Spurs, the Reds conceded three first half goals against a rampant Tottenham side who had title ambitions of their own. Fergie's men had already conceded 10 goals in their opening five league games and United fans started to fear the worst, as a heavy defeat seemed on the cards. However, comebacks had been synonymous with the Sir Alex Ferguson years and when Andy Cole pulled one back right after the restart, the champions started to kick into gear. Hope was restored just before the hour mark, when a Laurent Blanc header cut the deficit to one goal, after Beckham swung in another inch-perfect corner. Then two goals in six minutes by Ruud Van Nistelrooy and Juan Sebastian Veron put the Reds In front. David Beckham was once again part of a United team that had risen from the dead in biblical fashion and the term 'a game of two halves' had a new meaning. This confirmed that Fergie's team, that continued to be littered with the class of '92 graduates, were still capable of coming back from anything. David Beckham then made it 5-3 to United and held his arms aloft in jubilation. What started to look like a big win for Spurs, resulted in Beckham and the rest of his United team mates show-boating in the final few minutes, as the Reds ended-up winning 5-3.

David Beckham was one of United's own and despite his tumultuous journey with the media down the years, he still remained a United fan's favourite. Yet the opposition fans who targeted Beckham were still holding a grudge for a red card that happened three years previous. Moreover, the British press, including one national newspaper which printed a dart board with David Beckham's face on it, were still persisting with the continual witch-hunt. On October 6th 2001, everything changed in the blink of an eye in England's final World Cup qualifying game against Greece. England needed to win or draw the match to qualify outright for the World Cup, but were losing 2–1 with little time remaining. When Teddy Sheringham was fouled eight yards outside the Greek penalty area, England were awarded a free-kick and Beckham ensured England's qualification with a curling strike which resembled his trademark set-pieces for United over the years. Reconciliation had been made with those outside Old Trafford. Yet United's 'them against us' mentality which prospered so gloriously under Sir Alex Ferguson thus far, meant Beckham's performances seemed somewhat motivated by this philosophy prior to the England versus Greece match. Instead of being the villain on the international stage, he now became a hero and the nation saw United's number seven as the man who would be their saviour at the 2002 World Cup. If the vilification before his national reprieve was difficult for Beckham to deal with, then perhaps being the man who England pinned their hopes on to help them succeed in future tournaments was an even bigger burden to bear.

His form for United did not seem to be immediately affected by this as he scored in United's next game, which was a Champions League encounter against Olympiakos in a 2-0 win. His next goal came at Anfield, albeit in a 3-1 loss to Liverpool, which was amid a run of four defeats in five Premier League games for United. The Reds were in disarray and Beckham subsequently lost his place in the starting line-up and only started one of the next seven games.

Beckham ended the year on a personal high as he was voted the BBC Sports Personality of the Year for 2001, and he once again finished in second place in the F.I.F.A. World Player of the Year Awards, this time behind Luis Figo. This also coincided with a good run of form for United as they won twelve of their next thirteen league games. During this run on January 6th 2002, United played a dramatic F.A. Cup third round tie against Aston Villa, where Beckham was restored to the starting eleven. The Reds found themselves 2-0 down with thirteen minutes to go, but Solskjaer pulled one back for United before David Beckham set up Ruud Van Nistelrooy to power home the equaliser. Two minutes later, the Dutch striker scored the winner, which prompted a pitch invasion from the travelling United supporters, who had just witnessed another inconceivable comeback. This was perhaps the greatest cup tie that Beckham had been involved in since the famous F.A. Cup semi-final replay in 1999 against Arsenal. The scenes after this match echoed that game, as the Manchester United fans who flooded onto the pitch, carried David Beckham and Ruud Van Nistelrooy to the tunnel on their shoulders. Once again United's number seven was involved in another moment of the club's iconography.

Beckham's form picked up once more; and after setting up two of the three goals Solskjaer scored against Bolton in a 4-0 win on January 29th 2002, he then netted seven goals in his next ten games in all competitions. This run included two free-kicks, two penalties and two solo goals, however, the pick of the bunch came against West Ham United on March 16th 2002 when he delicately chipped the ball, whilst in full stride, into the Hammer's net from 20 yards. David Beckham's right foot had become so refined that he was now merely caressing the ball into the net from any distance. Just like his previous shirt owner Eric Cantona, the ball seemed to know what to do as soon as it touched his foot. The sphere of leather that curled, arced and spun after meeting his stellar boot moved as true as a the planets orbiting the stars in the cosmos. However if his outer-worldly skill on the pitch was winning him accolades, then off the pitch it appeared that the media were building the United number seven-up to fame that befitted planet Hollywood.

United's qualification to the quarter-finals of the Champions League saw them meet Deportivo Lacoruna over two legs. The first of these matches was away at Estadio de Riazor on April 2nd 2002. United had already lost twice to Deportivo in the group stages, yet it was the Reds who opened the scoring as David Beckham produced perhaps his best goal for Manchester United since he scored from the half-way line back in 1996. As the ball broke to him from over 30 yards out, the England captain looped the ball with pint-point accuracy over the stranded Jose Molina into the top corner of the net. Even by David Beckham's standards, who perhaps had the most glowing long-range goal scoring portfolio in football, this goal was nothing less than spectacular.

In the return leg on April 10th 2002 United won 3-2 to progress to the semi-finals, yet for Beckham, it was a bitter-sweet occasion. The United midfielder was injured during the match breaking the second metatarsal bone in his left foot. This meant that Beckham would miss the rest of 2001/2002 season and would struggle to regain full fitness for the impending World Cup in the summer.

The fact that the Reds had made it through to the semi-finals of the Champions League for the first time since the treble winning season seemed to take a back seat in the fall-out of the match, as it was Beckham's left foot that made the front page of the national newspapers. Many football fans were accustomed to seeing his face or Becks and his girlfriend on the front page, but now most people were all of a sudden amateur orthopaedicians and the metatarsal bone became familiar to those outside of medical school for the first time. As for United, their season faltered with elimination from Europe at the hands of Bayern Leverkusen. They then claimed a disappointing third place finish in the league, after defeat to Arsenal on the penultimate game of the Premier League season.

Beckham regained full fitness after returning from the World Cup in Japan and scored his first goal of the season for United on August 23rd 2002, with a curler into the top corner against Chelsea in a 2-2 draw at Stamford Bridge. He then produced another moment of dead-ball magic when he notched another classic Champions League goal with a long-range free-kick against Zalaegerszeg in United's next match. Beckham's appearances soon became limited after injuries saw Ole Gunnar Solskjaer replace him on the right side of midfield. Due to Solskjaer's good form, Beckham found it hard to win his place back in the starting eleven over the coming months. When Beckham did get his chance towards the end of the year he scored another long-range chip against Birmingham At Old Trafford in a 2-0 win, then set up another late comeback against Sunderland on New Year's Day when he equalised late on for the Reds, before they eventually won 2-1 in stoppage time with a winner from Scholes. He then made it three goals in a week after bending in another free-kick into the top left corner against Portsmouth in the F.A. Cup third round.

After United lost 2-0 to Arsenal in the fifth round of the F.A. Cup on February 15th 2003, The United number seven was seen wearing stitches above his left eye. It was an incident involving a flying boot in the changing room after Sir Alex Ferguson was disappointed with United's performance. The injury was later reported to be an accident; however, speculation arose over David Beckham's future at the club. Yet this did not appear to affect his performances, as he set up both goals in the next match against Juventus, first with a corner that was headed home by Wes Brown, then a long, weighted pass which was tucked away by Van Nistelrooy. He then set up a stoppage time equaliser which Solskjaer converted against Bolton in his next match, a late winner for Mikael Silvestre against Leeds at Old Trafford, before scoring a crucial winner in the title race during a 1-0 win Aston Villa, which closed the gap on leaders Arsenal.

Beckham did not start in some important games in the run-in, in particular the second leg of the Champions League quarter final against Real Madrid. After losing the first leg at the Bernabeau 3-1, United found themselves 3-2 down at Old Trafford, however, Beckham's introduction from the substitute's bench caused an immediate impact, as the United number seven scored one of the best free-kicks of his career before poaching a second goal minutes later.

United lost the match 6-5 on aggregate, none-the-less it was a credible performance against the holders of the competition.

Manchester United went on to win the Premier League after beating Charlton 4-1 with Beckham once again on the score sheet. United's last game of the season was against Everton at Goodison Park, where the one-time youth team player fittingly scored what turned out to be his last goal for Manchester United from a free-kick in a 2-1 win. Shortly after, David Beckham was awarded an Order of the British Empire for his services to football, before moving to Real Madrid in a £25 million transfer deal.

In his time at the club, he became arguably the greatest free-kick taker in the history of the sport. He revolutionised United's right-wing play, opting for guile and precision in his creativity over the traditional speed and trickery performed in that position. This allowed him to became the creator of United's most memorable moments during his time at the club. Yet he will be most fondly remembered by United fans for being part of the nucleus of youth players that helped Sir Alex Ferguson build a footballing empire; as the together with the great story of David Beckham's rise to fame, the simultaneous rise to stardom of all of Fergie's Fledglings is a fairytale in itself.

CRISTIANO RONALDO

Boss, you've got to sign this player.

On the August 6th 2003 Manchester United's pre-season fixture list saw them travel to Portugal for a friendly against Sporting Lisbon which commemorated the opening of the Alvalade XXI Stadium. That night, United lost 3-1 and it was the performance of an unknown eighteen-year-old that caught the eye of Sir Alex Ferguson. Yet this teenager was not one of his own players; he was instead playing in the green and white hoops of Sporting Lisbon. The young forward with the number 28 on his back terrorised the Red's defence for ninety minutes with such trickery and speed to the extent that several of the

Manchester United players urged the boss to sign him there and then. Sir Alex Ferguson and Manchester United had never acted in such a knee-jerk way as to purchase a player on the back of one performance. In fact the Portuguese whizz-kid had been monitored by United scouts for several months prior to this match and a deal was allegedly agreed on a verbal basis the night before the friendly. However, Cristiano Ronaldo's exhibition that night prompted the manager to confirm all the details of the move, as he knew that the teenager's wizardry would have alerted all of the elite clubs in Europe. The transfer fee cost £12.24 million and his signature made him Manchester United's first ever Portuguese player. Upon his arrival at Old Trafford, he requested the squad number 28, which was his old number at Sporting. However, Sir Alex Ferguson told him that he would be wearing the iconic number seven, despite knowing the pressure and expectation that was synonymous with the shirt.

Despite acquiring the signature of one of Europe's biggest prospects, it was generally believed that Ronaldo would be a player who United could nurture for the future. Cristiano even arrived at Manchester Airport the day after without any bags or clothing. Perhaps he was resigned to the idea that he would be loaned back to Sporting for his first season whilst on the books at Manchester United.

After Sir Alex Ferguson had sold David Beckham in the summer United fans were all guessing who his replacement would be. Even when United splashed out a then record fee for a teenager, there was no indication that he would fit straight into the team. However, Sir Alex Ferguson knew he had seen something special and all his players could talk about for days after the encounter was the eighteen-year-old, who had twisted the blood of the United defenders for 90 minutes. He was instantly given his introduction to English football on the opening day of the season which turned out to be one of the finest debuts ever seen at Old Trafford. His trickery mesmerised the Bolton defence and his skill had the crowd standing on their feet. Not since the days of George Best and Eric Cantona had anyone tantalised and entertained to this level of fantasy that the United fans perpetually yearn for. Never taking a backwards step, his mentality was just to attack, his feet were mesmeric and his balance and skill were making the Bolton defenders look like amateurs. When the boy was introduced as a substitute in the second half, you could forgive those who questioned whether Cristiano Ronaldo was good enough for the number seven shirt. The prevailing events on that day of August 13th 2003 had people wondering if the number seven shirt was good enough for Cristiano Ronaldo. He even earned United a penalty after a befuddled Bolton defence dragged him to the floor in desperation. The Reds eventually won 4-0, but the fans could only talk about one player, as a future star was unveiled at Old Trafford.

Sir Alex Ferguson, who was an avid protector of his young players, used Ronaldo sparingly in the first part of the 2003/2004 campaign. He did not become a regular starter until the final third of the season, however, his first goal for Manchester United came in the form of a free-kick at Old Trafford on the November 1st 2003. His whipped-in cross-come-shot bounced its way into the far corner of the net to secure a 3-0 win for the Reds against Portsmouth. The goal had a touch of fortuity about it, however, his unorthodox style of striking the ball from a dead position was on show for the first time; and there were early signs that he could take on the responsibility of set-pieces that was left behind by his number seven predecessor David Beckham. Ronaldo's next goal came in the F.A. Cup against Manchester City in an entertaining Derby match. United's new number seven scored their third goal in a 4-2 win at Old Trafford. Soon the young Portuguese winger was settling into life as a Manchester United player and a wonder strike against Tottenham Hotspur a few weeks later followed by two goals against Birmingham and Aston Villa showed glimpses of his potential.

None-the-less, it was not all plain-sailing for Ronaldo in his first season as a Manchester United player. Many critics accused the boy-wonder of being a one-trick pony. It was also suggested by those in football that the razzmatazz of his step overs and his ambitious attempts on goal were just a façade to mask the flaws of a physically weak player who had no end product.

Despite this, the manager had faith in his teenage sensation, and he dealt him the ultimate vote of confidence by starting him in the F.A. Cup final against Millwall. After ending the season on a bitter-sweet note, which saw him scoring a goal and seeing a red card in the last league match against Aston Villa, there became intrigue as to whether the nineteen-year-old could transfer his mesmerising dribbling skills and trickery onto the big stage. It did not take long before the Portuguese winger tore the hapless Millwall defence apart with a display of skill that was usually performed in an exhibition arena. Every party-piece he had learnt since growing up as a kid in Madeira was put on show. The icing on the cake was an F.A. Cup final goal just before half time when he headed in a Gary Neville cross to open the scoring for the Reds. United won 3-0 and Cristiano Ronaldo picked up his first piece of silverware at Manchester United.

The game itself proved that Ronaldo had all the attributes to be one of the greats at Old Trafford and that he could live up to the reputation of donning the sacred number seven jersey. After only eight minutes into the final, after beating his man on the touchline he sent in a cross by putting one leg behind the other and flicking the ball goalwards with his 'wrong' foot – a move contemporarily known as the 'Rabona'. Then after beating four players with a collection of flicks and tricks he found himself on the end of a two-footed lunge by Dennis Wise, who then clawed Ronaldo in the face with three other Millwall players surrounding him whilst he lay on the floor. This did not faze the teenager in the slightest. He was showing on the biggest stage that he could handle any kind of pressure and hostility. After being kicked from pillar to post by a rough and ready championship side, he then scored with a brave header. Evidently, United's new acquisition was no shrinking violet. This was not just another showboating youngster who would soon learn the harsh realities of professional football. This was the real deal; and where many thought his trickery was merely a masquerade for his footballing inadequacies, instead, on the contrary, it deflected the attention away from the evidence that he had the potential to become the most complete footballer in the land.

Cristiano Ronaldo's potential caught the eye of the Portuguese national coach Luiz Felipe Scolari and the United winger was included in the Portugal squad for the European Championships in 2004. This meant that he was given an extended rest after the tournament and was re-introduced a few weeks into the 2004/2005 season.

In terms of goal-scoring Ronaldo took a while to get out of the starting blocks and he had to wait until December 4th 2004 against Southampton in a 3-0 win to get off the mark. However, during the second part of the season the nineteen-year-old clicked into gear and after scoring in the previous year's final, the F.A. Cup became the main stage of choice to execute his talents. Soon his league form was also on the up and United's number seven saved his best performance of the season for a match at Highbury, against the previous year's 'Invincibles' Arsenal. This game will mainly be remembered for Roy Keane's verbal spat with Patrick Vieira in the tunnel before the game even started, however, it was a young Ronaldo and Rooney Partnership upfront that destroyed the reigning champions on their own turf. After going behind twice either side of a Ryan Giggs goal, Cristiano Ronaldo scored two quick fire goals to put United in front. Both goals had the air of an accomplished finisher as United won 4-2 on the night; and it was Cristiano Ronaldo's all-round performance that would grab the headlines the next day.

United had dropped too far off the championship pace going into the spring as Jose Mourinho's Chelsea were romping away with the league. Chelsea owner Roman Abramovic saw his millions deliver the London side instant success, yet Manchester United's team, with the inclusion of a teenage Ronaldo, was one for the future.

After Ronaldo scored in the third round of the F.A. Cup against Exeter, he then added to his cup tally with a goal in the fifth round against Everton and then another in the quarter-final against Southampton. A week after the last eight encounter in the cup, he then showed his spectacular side with a goal of the season contender against Fulham, where he beat two players before arrowing the ball into the top corner from twenty five yards. In their defence of the F.A. Cup, the holders now faced Newcastle in the semi-final at The Millennium Stadium, the ground where Manchester United and Ronaldo had won the cup during the previous season. Again the Portuguese youngster revelled in the spotlight and scored in a 4-1 rout over the Tynesiders.

United then returned to the Welsh capital for the final against Arsenal. The record books show that Arsenal won the trophy that year; however, Manchester United fans will remember this as one of the most one-sided matches that the Reds had ever lost. The team that went undefeated throughout the whole of the previous campaign were taught a lesson by United's teenage sensations Rooney and Ronaldo. Sir Alex Ferguson's team hit the woodwork twice and had a goal disallowed in normal time. They created chance after chance but failed to convert whilst limiting the Gunners to one attempt on goal, which came in the second period of extra time. Throughout the match, Arsenal defender Lauren committed several fouls on Cristiano Ronaldo, and confronted the Portuguese winger early in the second half, before finally being booked for persistent fouling in the 62nd minute. Then, with just seconds left in regulation time, Ronaldo made a break towards the Arsenal half, only to be cynically body-checked by Reyes. Referee Styles made no hesitation and showed Reyes a second yellow card, making the Spaniard the second player to be sent off in an FA Cup Final, after Manchester United's Kevin Moran in 1985. United eventually lost_on penalties after Paul Scholes failed to convert his spot-kick. The result was a hard one to take for Manchester United yet what they saw from Cristiano Ronaldo that day was another fearless performance. He terrorised Arsenal for 120 minutes, making a former invincible team look ordinary yet again.

The start of the 2005/2006 season began well for Ronaldo with a goal in the Champions League qualifiers in a 3-0 win against Debrecen at Old Trafford on August 9th 2005. However, soon his life was turned upside down when in early September that year, his Father passed away due to an alcohol related illness. Living in a foreign country so far away from home at a young age is a daunting prospect for any human being. However, this coupled with the loss of his father could make or break any footballer. The match following this tragic news was the Manchester Derby at Old Trafford on September 10th 2005. Ronaldo would take no part in this game on compassionate grounds.

By October the Reds had already fallen behind severely in the title race, with Chelsea once again pulling too far away at the top of the table. Their misery was compounded on the October 29th 2005 when they lost 4-1 away to Middlesbrough. None-the-less, Ronaldo's introduction into this match as a substitute on 60 minutes did bare some significance, as he netted Manchester United's 1000th Premier League goal with a consolation header in injury time.

United's league form going into the New Year was decent, although they had already perhaps lost too much ground on Jose Mourinho's Chelsea to mount a serious title challenge. Moreover, their Champion's League form was unimpressive and after winning only one group game out of their first five, they now had to travel to Benfica to get a result.

Ronaldo's return to Portuguese soil was never going to be an easy one, due to the fact that he previously played for Benfica's arch rivals Sporting Lisbon. During this game, the boos and the jeers badly affected his performance and United lost 2-1, which saw them crash out of the Champions League in the group stages for the first time since 1995. Cristiano Ronaldo was heavily criticised for his performance that night. He had proved that he could handle the big stage in England, yet his European pedigree as a top player was being questioned, as he had not scored in the Champions League proper in three seasons at the club. Subsequently, Ronaldo was left on the bench for the next three games, before returning to the starting line-up in the League Cup against Birmingham alongside many of United's fringe players.

Ronaldo started to make emends for his alleged downturn in form with two goals against Bolton wanderers on New Year's Eve. His second goal was more like the Ronaldo that everyone knew and loved. After receiving the ball on half-way, he then ran towards the goal whilst dazzling the Bolton defence with a series of step overs, before burying the ball in the bottom corner of the net.

Despite this, a generally disappointing season for the United number seven became worse, when he was sent-off in the Manchester Derby two weeks later in a 3-1 defeat at The City of Manchester Stadium. On a frustrating night for the Reds, Ronaldo felt aggrieved about several decisions that did not go his way. He decided to take action into his own hands by lunging at ex-United striker Andy Cole, and was duly shown a red card. This then followed a training session where it is alleged that Cristiano Ronaldo and Rudd van Nistelrooy had a bust-up over Ronaldo's apparent showboating. The Dutch striker vented his anger at Ronaldo's alleged lack of service that Van Nistelrooy used to enjoy from United's previous number seven David Beckham. Something had to give; and perhaps one of them had to go.

The one saving grace in the 2005/2006 season was the League Cup, where they reached the final to play Wigan Athletic after overcoming Blackburn in the last four. The Millennium Stadium in Cardiff was a ground which carried fond memories for Cristiano Ronaldo and interestingly Rudd van Nistelrooy was omitted from United's starting eleven at the expense of Louis Saha. After Scoring in the 2004 F.A. Cup final and the 2005 semi-final, then destroying Arsenal in the 2005 final at this stadium, there were high hopes for the Portuguese winger in Cardiff once more.

True to form, Ronaldo's love affair with these occasions continued against the newly-promoted Wigan side. United's number seven shone again in Cardiff when he was presented with a chance in the second half. After banging home a Louis Saha pass to make the score 3-0, the goal-scorer then ripped off his shirt in celebration. United went on to win 4-0 and Ronaldo picked up his second domestic winners medal to go with the one he won two years previous. The sub-story of that match was Sir Alex Ferguson leaving Ruud Van Nistelrooy as an unused substitute. The United manager instead introduced Kieron Richardson and new signings Nemanja Vidic and Patrice Evra from the bench, which perhaps showed where Fergie's allegiances lay in terms of picking his team. In a season of turmoil for Cristiano Ronaldo, perhaps his bright future had suddenly re-emerged at the expense of one of Manchester United's greatest ever strikers.

The Reds ended the season with a decent run in the league; however, they fell short at the expense of Chelsea with two games to go. Despite this, a second place finish to a team that had endless millions to spend on players was seen as progress after United's third place finish in the previous campaign. The attention now turned to the World Cup, Where Cristiano Ronaldo and Wayne Rooney were expected to be the young stars of the tournament. As fate would have it, Portugal met England in the quarter-final, which meant Ronaldo would now meet his fellow club teammate Rooney as an international opponent. The next chapter in a turbulent year of Ronaldo's Manchester United career took another twist when an hour into the game, it appeared that Wayne Rooney had stuck a boot on Portugal's Ricardo Carvalho. The replays were inconclusive as to whether it was intentional or not, however, Ronaldo proceeded to wave an imaginary card to the referee. The official that night Horacio Marcelo Elizondo then flashed a red card to Rooney; and as the England striker headed towards the tunnel, Ronaldo was caught winking towards the Portugal dugout. Rooney has never since blamed Ronaldo for getting him sent-off that day, however, the cynics in football were adamant that Ronaldo and Rooney could never play together again and believed that a move in the summer was imminent for Ronaldo.

The 2005/2006 season was a pivotal one for Ronaldo as his potential was still being questioned by those outside Manchester United. United's number seven should have still been classed as one of the brightest prospects in the game, yet those outside of Manchester United were still ridiculing his over-use of the step-over, his inability to stay on his feet when contact was made by an opponent and his apparent selfishness in front of goal. Those who saw him week-in-week-out at Old Trafford witnessed the rough-house treatment that the Portuguese winger received, many of which went unnoticed. This led to Ronaldo wanting to draw the referees attention to the persistent fouling, however, many saw this as unnecessary histrionics. Something had to happen as Ronaldo's lack of protection from referees coupled with his lightweight frame meant that despite his bravery, English football could kick him out for good - quite literally.

Yet just like with every legend of the number seven, there comes a time when they all hit a low point in their football career. George Best's off-the-field stardom and champaign lifestyle was overlooked by Sir Matt Busby because he knew his performances on the field could take the Reds to heights that have never been reached before. Bryan Robson's injury record and involvement in United's drinking culture of the eighties was accepted due to the inspirational captain's ability to drag his team to achieve silverware, in an era when Liverpool monopolised the end of season spoils. Eric Cantona played on the edge of sanity with simmering blood, which redefined the landscapes of possibility for Sir Alex Ferguson, with the boss knowing the Frenchman could fall over that edge at any given time. David Beckham's pop stardom lifestyle was tolerated throughout his peak because his incessant practicing meant that his crossing and shooting had almost reached perfection. Cristiano was no different to his number seven predecessors. The heir to the famous jersey had undoubtedly now hit his lowest point as a United player, however, just as Cantona was welcomed back with unconditional love from the fans after his ban and Beckham was received with open arms after his World Cup red card, Ronaldo was promised by Sir Alex Ferguson that he would get the same treatment at the Theatre of Dreams following the winking incident at the World Cup in 2006.

From Boy to Man

Something happened to Cristiano Ronaldo that summer. He returned to the United line-up on the first day of the 2006/2007 season mentally and physically a man. The death of his father and the events at the World Cup had encouraged him to a new-found maturity. The boy who had been bullied by the Premier League's hatchet men in the previous three seasons had now become physically superior to the majority of the league. He returned as the ultimate athlete with an end product to his flashy showmanship. He strutted around Old Trafford barrel-chested with an arrogance that was justified; and instead of players knocking him off the ball, players bounced off him instead.

He had come a long way since his debut in 2003, where he appeared as a spotty teenager with blonde highlights, whose shirt hung off his gangly frame. His timid yet flashy footwork had now changed into a powerful gazelle-like stride. This time he had a purpose, and he vowed to his teammates during the summer of 2006 that he would become the best player in the world.

Any questions regarding Ronaldo's relationship with Rooney were soon put to bed on the opening day of the 2006/2007 season. United hammered Fulham 5-1 after Ronaldo and Rooney put in a blistering performance with both players ending up on the score sheet. Ronaldo's consistency went from sporadic to almost perfect this season with the Portuguese star scoring and assisting in nearly every game. After hammering in another eye-defying solo effort against Reading, he then went on a run which saw him score twelve goals before Christmas, including six goals in three matches in December against Wigan, Reading and Aston Villa respectively. This meant that Ronaldo had already equalled his total for the whole of the last campaign.

United's number seven now proved he had an end product to go with his bag of tricks, however, some critics still suggested that he failed to produce in the big games. This was on the basis that he had not scored against any of the top four teams in England, nor had he netted a single goal in the Champions League. The final stretch of the 2006/2007 saw United facing stern challenges at home and abroad; and Cristiano Ronaldo would again be under the spotlight.

The Reds went into February six points clear of Chelsea at the top of the league, however, going three years without the Premier League trophy heaped immense pressure on the team to hold out until the end of the season. Despite their point's advantage, they still had a tough run-in and they still had to play Jose Mourinho's side at Stamford Bridge. On February 24th 2007 United looked like faltering again after going behind to Fulham at Craven Cottage. Although Ryan Giggs had equalised, Fulham continued to bombard United's goal and it took several saves from Edwin Van der Sar and the United woodwork to keep the scores level. With two minutes to go and United looking like the also-rans of the last three years, Cristiano Ronaldo picked the ball up in his own half. After beating two players on the by-line he cut inside towards the box, turned the Cottagers' defence inside out and scored the goal that kept United in pole-position. The Fulham defence was as shredded as the nerves of the fans and the players. The United number seven then ran to the dugout and jumped on teammate Gabriel Heinze, before the rest of the United team swamped Ronaldo in jubilation. Soon the boy wonder started to show why he was now being labelled the best player in Europe and the team's reaction painted an elaborate picture. Not since the dramatic scenes against Sheffield Wednesday in 1993 when Steve Bruce's header sparked a touchline frenzy had we seen such celebrations. These scenes only occur when a team starts to believe they can win the league; and maybe this flash of genius gave the players the belief that with Cristiano Ronaldo in the side, anything could happen.

A week later against Liverpool, United had their backs against the wall again. Playing Liverpool at Anfield is a tall order in any circumstances, yet playing with ten men made the task even harder. After Paul Scholes saw red for lashing out at Xabi Alonso, United looked like holding on for a point. It then took a wonder save from

Van der Sar off a Peter Crouch shot to keep the scores level. As the game ticked into injury time the Reds won a free-kick on the Edge of the Liverpool box. Ronaldo, who in the past had a tendency to make the wrong choices, now had a do-or-die mission to create a goal. The Portuguese winger sent in a wicked ball which was impossible to defend and difficult for the goalkeeper to keep hold of. The ball eventually squirted out to John O'Shea who smashed in a dramatic winner. Ronaldo was involved again in late drama for the second time in a week and the United players and fans celebrated like they had already won the championship.

Soon United's attention turned to the F.A. Cup and the Champions League. The Reds booked a place in the Semi-Final of the F.A. Cup after winning a replay against Middlesbrough 1-0, with Ronaldo converting a late winner from the penalty spot. The Portuguese star also scored in the first match which resulted in a 2-2 draw. Then after beating Lille over two legs in the last 16 of the Champions League, they now faced Roma in the quarter-final.

After the Reds were beaten 2-1 in the first leg in Rome, Sir Alex Ferguson appeared surprisingly optimistic coming into this game as Rooney's away goal, despite having ten men, meant that United had given themselves a lifeline. As it turned out, United plundered seven goals past a shell-shocked Roma side. The Reds were 4-0 up at half time and Cristiano Ronaldo scored his first two Champions league goals in a United jersey. This together with goals from Smith, Rooney, Evra and a brace from Michael Carrick meant that with a 7-1 score-line, United had won by the biggest margin in the knock-out stages of the Champions League and to Fergie's own admission, this was the finest European night ever to be staged at Old Trafford. Ronaldo was now reproducing his domestic form on the European stage. The memories of the previous season's exit, where the blame lay heavily on Ronaldo's shoulders, was now a distant memory.

Four day later the Reds beat Watford 4-1 in the F.A. Cup semi-final at Villa Park, with Ronaldo amongst the scorers yet again. Their place in the final had been secured, however, the Premier League still had to be sewn-up and a Champions League semi-final against AC Milan was next on the European agenda. United made a dream start at Old Trafford in the first leg against Milan with Ronaldo scoring a header after only five minutes on the clock. There was now no occasion too big for the Portuguese colossus, who was beginning to stand head and shoulders above the rest. Despite this, United's decimated defence which had no Vidic or Ferdinand conceded two sloppy goals, both of which were scored by Kaka. United eventually won 3-2 after two goals from Rooney, which included an injury time winner, yet the two away goals for Milan gave United a difficult task in the second leg.

Four days later on April 28th 2007 the Reds now faced a crunch league game against Everton at Goodison Park. Ronaldo was left on the bench for this game, as the manager tried to keep his key players fresh for the second leg of the Champions League semi-final in Italy. After a sluggish start which saw United trailing by two goals with half-an-hour to play, United pulled one back, which was Sir Alex Ferguson's cue to ask Ronaldo to warm up. His impact was immediate as a towering header forced Phil Neville to convert the ball into his own net. United's number seven was then instrumental in the rest of United's 4-2 comeback, which left United on the brink of Premier League glory.

Ecstasy soon turned to disappointment as the Reds crashed out of the Champions League with a 3-0 defeat to AC Milan at the San Siro. After being a couple of wins away from another unprecedented treble, United had to put the European disappointment behind them, as their attention now turned to domestic glory. Three days after the Milan defeat, Fergie's men faced Manchester City in the Premier League. In a dour game at Eastlands, it was the red half of Manchester who were celebrating as Cristiano Ronaldo stepped-up to score the winning goal from the penalty spot. This turned out to be the title winning goal for Manchester United as Chelsea could only draw with Arsenal the following day. This secured their sixteenth League title, with Cristiano Ronaldo finishing as the joint-top scorer with Wayne Rooney, having netted 23 goals in all competitions.

The Reds then failed to secure the double after losing in extra-time to Chelsea in the F.A. Cup at Wembley, however, they had re-asserted themselves as the top dogs in England once more after watching three years of Arsenal and Chelsea dominance.

Ballon D'Or

Cristiano Ronaldo had an indifferent start to the 2007/2008 campaign after receiving a red card against Portsmouth during the second game of the season. United's number seven was banned for the following three league matches, before his season was up-and-running after netting another trademark header against his former club Sporting Lisbon in the Champions League. Ronaldo refused to celebrate and looked almost apologetic after the goal, on a night which was an emotional return for the Portuguese star. On the same ground where the young winger caught the attention of everyone at Manchester United with his virtuoso performance in a friendly, Ronaldo showed the up most respect to the fans who watched him make his professional debut as a footballer.

Last season's top scorer then clicked in to prolific goal scoring form with another piece of individual brilliance against Birmingham City in the league on September 29th 2007, which sealed United's fifth 1-0 win of the season. He then scored against table-toppers Arsenal in a 2-2 draw at The Emirates Stadium.

Ronaldo's free-kick taking during this season became one of the winger's most dangerous weapons. In United's home tie during the group stages of the Champions League against Sporting Lisbon, Ronaldo stood over a free-kick thirty-five yards from goal. The Reds still needed a win to secure the top-spot in the group, and with 90 minutes up on the clock, it was down to United's number seven again to win the match with only seconds remaining. With one punt of his majestic right boot, the ball whistled into the corner of the net to seal all three group points for the Reds.

Cristiano then went on a run that saw him score eighteen times before the New Year, which included braces against Wigan, Dynamo Kiev, Blackburn, Fulham and Everton. Then on Boxing Day against Sunderland he scored another free-kick with a seemingly impossible trajectory, as the ball rocketed over the wall and into the net before the goalkeeper could even move.

Last year's top scorer then scored his first ever hat-trick for Manchester United in a 6-0 demolition of Newcastle United at Old Trafford. After scoring two goals in a game on thirteen previous occasions for the Reds, Ronaldo went one better with a couple of individual goals and a free-kick. This time the set-piece was an innovative under-the-wall trick which saw the Newcastle defence jump over his shot. The Portuguese winger had now scored 22 goals by the second week of January.

Then on January 30th 2008 Cristiano Ronaldo completely proved that he had reinvented the art of free-kick taking for good when he discarded the old 'Beckham' like curlers for the more modern day practice of hitting the ball with his boot laces. After scoring several improbable free-kicks previously, Ronaldo soon became confident that he could score from anywhere. However, because of the way he struck the ball, with the position of this free-kick against Portsmouth it seemed impossible to hit the target. The Portuguese winger wearing the blood red shirt of Manchester United with the iconic number seven on his back knew that impossible meant nothing. He stood there in his gun-slinger stance, then strode up to the ball and somehow bent it up and over the Portsmouth wall as if it had a heat-seeking missile attached to the back. The ball arrowed into the top corner of David James's goal and the best defences of Europe stood up and realised that Cristiano Ronaldo's artillery contained the best free-kick of modern times.

Just like the days of Eric Cantona, it was the number seven of the 2007/2008 season Cristiano Ronaldo that was finding a flash of genius to win games out of nothing. When fixtures were coming thick and fast and the hard slog of a long season was taking its toll on the players, United's talisman dug deep his into his repertoire to almost single-handedly win football matches. After scoring the only goal of the second leg of the Champion's League last-sixteen match against Lyon, which booked United's passage into the quarter-final, Ronaldo then scored a late winner against Derby in another 1-0 win. This was followed by a brace against Bolton in the league, before a match against Aston Villa on March 29th 2008.

Cristiano Ronaldo has the most complete repertoire of goals in world football, however, for a player of his calibre the portfolio cannot be finished unless you back flick the ball through an opponent's leg to score a goal. This is exactly what Ronaldo did when the ball broke to him in the penalty area from a corner and so his scrapbook became complete. Prior to this match he had scored impossible free-kicks, long-range efforts, solo goals, volleys and headers, but none of them were as innovative and cheeky as this back-heal in the 4-0 thrashing of Aston Villa at Old Trafford. This was the Portuguese winger's 26th league goal of the season, but United's number seven did not stop there. Either side of this goal, Ronaldo powered home a header in the league against Liverpool at Old Trafford and then swept home the opening goal against Middlesbrough in a 2-2 draw at snow swept Riverside Stadium.

On April 1st 2008 United faced Roma for the second year running in the quarter-finals of the Champions League. The sign of a great player is one that can get kicked and then get up and carry on. Ronaldo showed these characteristics week in week out, and his bravery was one of his finer attributes, which was repeatedly overlooked by the critics. His aerial ability was also another part of his game that was constantly overlooked, however, in the cauldron of Roma's Stadio Olimpico he killed two birds with one stone as he scored one of the greatest headers ever seen. Paul Scholes crossed the ball into the box and despite the imminent danger from the Roma defence, the ball smashed the back of the net off Ronaldo's forehead. The momentum of his towering leap caused the Portuguese star to clatter into a defender and take a blow to the head. The winger was shaken but took the incident in his stride, he then continued to play a vital role in United securing a 2-0 win despite the hostile conditions and helped United put one foot into the semi-finals of the Champions League.

United won the return leg 1-0 to book a place against Barcelona in the last four. In between these matches, Ronaldo scored the equalising penalty in a 2-1 win over Arsenal at Old Trafford. It was evident from an early age that pressure was one thing that did not phase Cristiano Ronaldo, so when he had to re-take a penalty against Arsene Wenger's side at Old Trafford in a potential title decider, he showed no signs of faltering, after netting the second penalty in the same corner as the first one, which was originally ruled out for encroachment.

He was then charged with the task of taking another penalty, this time at the Nou Camp against European giants Barcelona. In the opening minutes of the semi-final first leg, United were awarded a spot-kick after a Barcelona player handled the ball in the area. Ronaldo stepped up with his usual brimming confidence; however, the Portuguese star blazed his effort wide of the goal. Many saw this as a missed opportunity to return to the Champions League final for the first time since 1999 and it meant the Reds now had to beat Barcelona at Old Trafford. To the relief of the Portuguese winger, United beat the Spanish champions 1-0 with a Paul Scholes goal to reach the final in an emotional year for the club. Ronaldo had been reprieved and with Fergie's men needing two wins from their remaining two league games to win the title, United's wing wizard stepped-up to the mark with two goals against West Ham in a 4-1 win at Old Trafford, before converting a penalty away to Wigan on the final day of the season to secure a second Premier League title in a row. The Reds now turned their attention to the Champions League final against Chelsea.

50 years after the Munich air disaster, United found themselves involved in another historic football match. United's number seven had finished the league campaign as top scorer and the Portuguese star had already claimed the Golden Boot award, plus he was the firm favourite for the Ballon D'Or. United's hopes of winning their third European Cup were placed firmly at the feet of their number seven, however, it was his head that stole the headlines in the biggest ever game involving two British clubs. In a first half of United dominance, Ronaldo opened the scoring after he towered above the Chelsea defence to plant a trademark header past a stranded Petr Cech from a Wes Brown cross. Just before the break the ball then broke kindly for Frank Lampard and the game was locked at 1-1. This lifted the Chelsea team and subsequently they looked like the more likely winners as they twice hit the woodwork, yet sometimes destiny is a force that cannot be beaten.

There was no resolution in extra-time so the game was to be decided on penalties. After Ronaldo missed his spot-kick, John Terry, the captain of Chelsea, strutted to the penalty spot knowing he was one kick away from lifting the Champions League. All of a sudden Sir Alex had to rely on his old friend, fate. As United fans closed their eyes, as their hearts pumped the red of Manchester United around their souls, as the game entered the day that George Best was born, in the match that Ryan Giggs broke Bobby Charlton's appearance record and as Sir Matt and the Busby Babes looked down from the gates of football heaven, John Terry miraculously slipped and the ball just seemed to be repelled by Edwin Van der Sar's goal mouth before hitting the post and going wide. The momentum switched in favour of United and after Ryan Giggs had put them ahead in sudden death, Edwin Van der Sar saved Nicolas Anelka's penalty to claim Sir Alex Ferguson's second Champions League trophy as manager of Manchester United. As the rest of Ronaldo's teammates ran towards the Dutch keeper, the goal-scorer broke down in tears in the middle of the pitch.

Ronaldo had reached his potential and the 42 goals he scored in the 2007/2008 season helped guide United to the Holy Grail of European success. His vow to become the best player in the world proved to be true. Moreover he proved that he could live up to the reputation of wearing the historic number seven shirt at Manchester United. The question remained, how long could United keep Ronaldo in this iconic jersey? The rumours were rife during the summer that Cristiano Ronaldo would move to Real Madrid, however, perhaps it was the temptation of playing in a World Club Championship that kept the world's best player in the number seven shirt of Manchester United.

After missing the first part of the 2008/2009 season through injury, which unfortunately included a 2-1 defeat in the European Super Cup Final against Zenit St. Petersburg, Ronaldo made his first full start in the League Cup against Middlesbrough where he scored another header in a 3-1 win. This was followed by eight goals in his next eleven games which included double strikes against Wets Ham United, Hull City and then two free-kicks against Stoke City, the first of which was his 100th goal for the club. The Ballon D'Or winner was showing the form that won him the award during the previous season and with a heavy fixture schedule that included a trip to Japan in December, United's number seven would have to remain at the top of his game. The Reds faced Gamba Osaka in the semi-final of the World Club Cup where Ronaldo scored a classic header in in a 5-3 win. United then became world champions for the second time in their history with a 1-0 win over LDU Quito after Ronaldo set up Wayne Rooney to score the winner.

There was nothing left to fill on Cristiano Ronaldo's résumé at Old Trafford, however, there was still plenty to play for in the 2008/2009 season. The player who came to Manchester United to prove he was the best in the world, now knew he was the best. Instead of playing to be the number one in his profession, he was playing as the number one. His swagger did not wane and his step-overs still baffled defenders. He was the most gifted player on earth, receiving the most exposure in the process, yet the opposition still had not figured him out. Despite his fame, he remained enigmatic with his skill. Most defenders could predict what was coming from the Portuguese wizard, yet they were too powerless to prevent it from happening. Defensive walls could not stop his free-kicks, ordering two defenders to mark him could not prevent his penetrative runs into the box. This was no longer exhibition stuff from Ronaldo; it was now a force that could not be stopped. The tricks and flicks that were once ridiculed by his critics were now taking the game to a new level and nothing could get in his way. He was the complete footballer, a modern day prototype that all footballers had to aspire to.

On January 20th 2009 Ronaldo scored in the second leg of the League Cup semi-final in a 4-2 win over Derby County which booked United a place in the final after losing the first leg 1-0. This was followed by two goals away to West Bromwich Albion in a 5-0 victory, then a winning penalty against Everton at Old Trafford. Another wonder free-kick from an acute angle against Blackburn Rovers kept United on course in the title-hunt, before they faced a nitty-gritty end to the season with the Reds still firing in all four competitions.

United's passage into the last eight of the Champions League was confirmed when they beat Jose Mourinho's Inter Milan 2-0 on aggregate, with both goals coming at Old Trafford where Ronaldo headed in the second after Vidic's opener. Their Premier League campaign, however, took a serious knock-back when the Reds lost two games in a row. First to Liverpool at Old Trafford in a shock 4-1 defeat, where Ronaldo scored United's only goal from the penalty spot, then against Fulham at Craven Cottage by a 2-0 score-line. The Reds then had to dig deep when they were losing to Aston Villa in their next league match. After Ronaldo opened the scoring, United found themselves 2-1 down with ten minutes to play. Soon they were looking like they had run out of ideas and their dreams of a third Premier League trophy appeared to be in tatters. However, Ronaldo equalised on 80 minutes, before Frederico Macheda netted the injury time winner in one of the most dramatic games in United's history.

Ronaldo then had the daunting prospect of a return to his homeland in the second leg of the Champions League quarter-final against Porto. United went into this European game knowing nothing more than a win would do, after their disappointing 2-2 draw in the first leg at Old Trafford against the Portuguese outfit. Before the game, people were calling for Cristiano Ronaldo to stand up and be counted on his return to Portugal and prove to the nation why he was the reigning Ballon D'Or holder. With Cristiano not being one to turn down a challenge, the United winger scored what turned out to be the goal of the season. After picking the ball up in the Porto half, Ronaldo unleashed a shot from an impossible distance that exploded of his right boot from 40 yards. Despite the distance, the Porto goalkeeper had no chance of saving it, as the ball astonishingly rattled the top corner of the net and later Ronaldo described it as "The best goal I have ever scored". United's number seven had taken his goal-scoring capabilities to a new height and it also proved to be the winner which booked United a place in the semi-final.

Four days later Sir Alex Ferguson's dream of a quadruple was stopped in its tracks after losing to Everton on penalties in the semi-final of the F.A. Cup. Yet their league form returned to its usual consistency, with United winning seven games on the trot after their blip against Liverpool and Fulham. Amid this run was a semi-final Champions League tie against Arsenal.

On May 5th 2009 the Reds took a slender 1-0 lead to the Emirates in the second leg of this semi-final, yet after they squandered several opportunities in the first leg at Old Trafford, Arsenal believed that United had missed the chance to put themselves into the final. However Cristiano Ronaldo had other ideas as first his trickery on the left wing set up Ji-Sung Park to open the scoring and then three minutes later he smashed in a forty yard free-kick that no other player on the planet would even attempt. Arsenal now needed four goals and the game was effectively over, but for United the best was yet to come. After clearing an Arsenal corner, United started one of the greatest counter-attacks ever seen when Park ran clear from the Gunner's defence. After a one two with Ronaldo, he then played in Rooney who's first time ball found United's number seven in the box, after the magician from Madeira ran the length of the field to meet it. He then powered the ball into the roof of the net. United tore Arsenal apart with counter-attacking football from another planet and Cristiano Ronaldo was the orchestrator of it all, in what was arguably his finest display in a Manchester United shirt. The Reds ran-out 3-1 winners, however, on another day it could have easily been six or seven.

United then all but sealed their third Premier League title in a row after a 2-0 win over Manchester City where Ronaldo netted another free-kick before lifting the Premier League trophy for the third year in a running, after a goalless draw with Arsenal at Old Trafford.

Sir Alex Ferguson then led his team out for the second Champions League final in a row, this time against Barcelona in Rome, with Ronaldo at the forefront of the attention yet again. The final was built-up to be the Ronaldo versus Messi show, and for the first ten minutes, it looked like Ronaldo had the upper hand. However, once Samuel Eto'o opened the scoring for Barcelona it became a tall order for the Reds. Lionel Messi then confounded Manchester United's and Cristiano Ronaldo's misery by scoring a second and the Spanish side were crowned the Champions of Europe.

Despite this disappointment, Cristiano Ronaldo had now scored in every major final for United, won every major trophy, won Young Player of the Year, Player's Player of the Year, Football Writer's Player of the Year, European Player of the Year and had been the Premier League's top scorer plus the top scorer in Europe. That night in Moscow in 2008 he established himself as one of the greatest players ever to have played for Manchester United before becoming the first Ballon D'Or winner since the 'Holy Trinity' of Best, Law and Charlton. The disappointment of the 2009 final did not diminish Ronaldo as an idolised figure at Old Trafford. His emergence from a lightweight teenager who knew a few tricks to the best footballer on the planet was a meteoric rise that befitted anyone wearing the number seven shirt at Manchester United. His legendary status still remains at the Theatre of Dreams and United fans continue to sing 'Viva Ronaldo' to this day.

Notable Mentions

The first match that Manchester United's founder club Newton Heath LYR played in a major competition was in the 1986/87 season, when they faced Fleetwood Rangers in the F.A. Cup first round. Although numbers were not allocated in those days, the man who would be most likely to be given the number seven shirt according to his position would have been John Earp, who played in the outside-right position that day.

The first superstar that could be attributed to the number seven role in the days that preceded shirt numbering was Billy Meredith. The man known as the 'Welsh Wizard' joined United in 1906 and remained their until 1921, playing for 15 years mainly in the outside-right position. He was known as one of the early stars of football due to his dribbling skills and all-round wing-play and he had the persona to match, as he was quite often seen chewing on a toothpick whilst strutting up and down the touch-line. Meredith helped United win two First Division titles and an F.A. Cup during his time at the club, where he scored 36 goals in 335 appearances.

In 1951 United signed outside right Johnny Berry from Birmingham City for £15,000. Berry then became one of Matt Busby's stars of the 50's, with his dibbling and crossing in the number seven shirt being a menace for many opposition defenders. He became one of only two United players, along with Roger Byrne, to appear in all three of United's Division One winning seasons during this decade.

After United's first league success under Busby, the manager then opted for youth over experience, meaning many of the senior players made way for the legendary Busby Babes. Yet Berry kept his place in the team and was an integral part of perhaps one of the greatest English sides ever, as United won back-to-back league titles, before venturing into Europe for the first time.

Berry then survived the Munich Air Disaster in 1958, where the injuries he sustained ended his playing career at the age of 31. Due to amnesia after the crash, Berry had no memory of the tragic incident and was unaware that some of his teammates had died. During his two month stay in hospital, Berry was said to be upset that his good friend Tommy Taylor had not visited him, oblivious to the fact that Taylor had sadly died in Munich.

After the disaster, Manchester United needed to sign several replacements at short notice to field a team for their impending fixtures. One of the clubs willing to help was Bishop Auckland, who loaned three of their players to United, including outside right, Warren Bradley. United's new number seven impressed Matt Busby that much that he was signed as part-time professional. Bradley, who also had a teaching job in Stretford, was then selected for the England national team in May 1959, where he scored two goals during a tour of North America. This meant that the United number seven was the only player in history to appear for the England amateur team and the England professional team in the same season.

After two seasons with Bradley playing predominantly in this number, it was then shared between Dawson, Giles, Quixall and Setters before the emergence of George Best. After Best had left the club, the next player to nail down the position of right-winger and, in turn, the number seven shirt was Steve Coppell, who was signed from Tranmere Rovers in 1975. Coppell was a part of Tommy Docherty's cup specialists in the late 70's, where he won an F.A. Cup winners medal against Liverpool in 1977. The tricky winger then went on to break the record for the most consecutive appearances for an outfield player at Manchester United, whilst making 207 starts in a row for the Reds between 1977 and 1981. Again another record attributed to a player in the number seven position.

Since Ronaldo abdicated the number seven throne in 2009, the shirt has become a hot potato due to both fear and prestige. The players who have been allocated the number seven shirt since that day have been put under intense scrutiny from both the fans and the media, as they are constantly expected to live up to the precedent set by the previous owners. The ardent idolaters that await the sixth coming of a player of messianic ability have shown a mixture of dubiousness and over-exaltation towards any recipient of the jersey, causing any player to wear the number with great trepidation.

Michael Owen was a player with a resume to fit the bill, as winning the Ballon D'Or in 2001 meant he possessed the highest individual honours in the game. Although he arrived with the same criteria as previous number sevens George Best and Cristiano Ronaldo, who achieved this feat whilst wearing the number seven shirt of Manchester United, Owen was in a stage of his career where his best days were behind him. Furthermore, many fans felt that his association with Liverpool would tarnish any reputation that the striker could build at Old Trafford. It was perhaps going to take something big for the England striker to win the affections of the supporters, which at this point in his life seamed a notion that was way beyond the realms of possibility. However on September 20th 2009, Manchester United faced Manchester City at Old Trafford, in a game that was supposed to represent a power shift in Mancunian superiority between the two clubs.

The match was also hyped up by the return of Tevez to Old Trafford, who decided to switch allegiances to the blue side of Manchester over the summer, with Owen being recruited on a free transfer as his replacement. A pulsating first half finished 1-1 with Wayne Rooney's opener being cancelled out by Gareth Barry after a slip by keeper Ben Foster. Soon after the restart Darren Fletcher headed United infront, only for Craig Bellamy to equalise from long range. In the closing stages United bombarded the City goal and after several attempts were thwarted by an inspired Shay Given, another Fletcher header looked like giving United all three points, but a mistake from Rio Ferdinand in the 90th minute gifted Bellamy his second and City's third goal of the game making the score 3-3.

United hung their heads in despair as Mark Hughes's men had somehow earned a draw and City's travelling fans celebrated as if they had won the league. However, there was twist in the tale, a twist so dramatic that the fairy tale writers hung up their quills for good. The new United number seven Michael Owen who once donned the Liverpool jersey, now became an honorary Mancunian by sliding home a 96th minute winner to silence the team who Sir Alex Ferguson dubbed the 'noisy neighbours'. This meant that although Owen would perhaps never be considered a true legend of the number seven, he had carved himself firmly into the tablets of Manchester United folklore.

Antonio Valencia joined the club in 2009 as cover for Cristiano Ronaldo, who was transferred in the summer of that year to Real Madrid. He then made the transition from a squad number of 25 to the legendary number seven shirt at the start of the 2012/13 season, after three very productive season's as a Manchester United right-winger. This seemed to have a detrimental effect on the Ecuadorian's performances, as although United won the league that year, Valencia's contribution of one goal in 40 matches followed by what the winger considered to be a below par season for him prompted Valencia to relinquish the shirt. By his own request he has now reverted back to his old squad number of 25, as the burden of being a Manchester United number seven was perhaps too heavy for such a reserved and humble footballer.

The number seven shirt remained vacant for the 2013/14 season, as it had now become a number which was reserved for a big name signing and symbol of hope that the next saviour would be on his way to Old Trafford. Following the retirement of Sir Alex Ferguson, new manager David Moyes seemed hopeful of filling this void, however, the marquee signing that he hoped for did not materialise. This meant that the following season, the new boss Louis Van Gaal was able to acquire the signature of Angel Di Maria, a footballer who was considered to be in the world class bracket and an ideal candidate to fill the shirt. Yet once again the hopes did not live up to the reality, as a the Argentinian winger did not hit the lofty heights that he achieved at Real Madrid, which saw him win the man of the match award in their 4-1 European Cup Final win over Atletico Madrid in the previous season. The following season Louis Van Gaal then opted for a fellow Dutchman and Eredivisie whiz-kid Memphis De Pay, who's potential rather than current stature was touted to eventually fulfil the expectations of the shirt, however his move to Lyon in 2017 has since left the current number seven shirt vacant for the next recipient.

A Note From the Author

The things that you notice when you make your first visit to a football game are quite often the smallest and most obscure observations. The smell of burger vans and the scripted yelling of the fanzine sellers on route to the stadium is prominent because these occur to the senses when you are at your most excited. Upon entry to the ground you feel the tension in the chatter and din of the fans who are stood in the half-way house of football spectating, which is the vacant space underneath the terraces where you can buy your programme and pre-match drinks. Then the most bizarre phenomenon is when you first walk up the stairs to your seating or standing area. For me, firstly, it was how wide the pitch looked. Upon looking down on the turf and its markings, it appeared that the golden ration theory had been thrown in to the Irwell, as the strip of green seemed more square than than the rectangular perception that is beamed from our television sets.

The audio of the atmosphere had an unusual echo which is not consistent with how you imagine the sound to be like at a football match. Clapping and applause had a squeaky reverberation and the smell of Bovril, tea and cigarette smoke became strangely comforting. The terrace below looked like a stirring pot of red rice pudding, just like the school dinners of the 80's and 90's when you mixed the spoonful of jam into a bowl of the stuff. Then the players lined-up in perfect lines across the pitch in the favoured 4-4-2 formation of the time. It was perplexing how they could achieve this at ground level, yet it was admirable from a birds eye view in the K-Stand. These lines were never broken, and they almost seemed to be bound together like the figurines on the poles of a table football set.

Then on December 6th 1992 these poles may have well been snapped, and the old table football set now had to be put back in the loft. For the first time since watching Manchester United from the stands, the impressive and regimented lines of men in red had been broken after 45 minutes of this match. The substitute who was wearing the number twelve shirt was distorting the aesthetics of the choreography and was stood in a positional anomaly amongst the usual linearity. At no point was Eric Cantona in a set position, he had broken the mould, both metaphorically and literally. I was dazzled by this rebellion and non-conformity and in awe of his unwitting refusal to man his position. There was no such thing as looking at a 4-4-2 formation anymore from those in an elevated view; it was the closest thing to post-modernism that English football had ever experienced. From that day, just as the terraces, Bovril and cigarette smoke started to disappear from a match day, so did Manchester United's doubts about winning the Premier league title.

24387861R00088

Printed in Great Britain
by Amazon